STILL GROWING
STILL LEARNING
STILL ME

STILL GROWING STILL LEARNING STILL ME

A Journey of Protest, Healing, and Personal Transformation

KENNY STILLS

BROOKLYN, NEW YORK
Publishing books since 1997

Still Growing, Still Learning, Still Me is the latest title in Dave Zirin's Edge of Sports imprint. Addressing issues across many different sports at both the professional and nonprofessional/collegiate levels, Edge of Sports aims to provide an even deeper articulation about the daily collision between sports and politics, giving cutting-edge writers the opportunity to fully explore their areas of expertise in book form.

Published by Edge of Sports/Akashic Books
©2026 Kenny Stills

All photographs courtesy of Kenny Stills unless credited otherwise.

ISBN: 978-1-63614-274-6
Library of Congress Control Number: 2025941006

All rights reserved
First printing

EU Authorized Representative details:
Easy Access System Europe
Mustamäe tee 50, 10621 Tallinn, Estonia
gpsr.request@easproject.com

Edge of Sports
c/o Akashic Books
Brooklyn, New York, USA
Instagram, Facebook, X: AkashicBooks
info@akashicbooks.com
www.akashicbooks.com

TABLE OF CONTENTS

Preface: Soul Rebel   *11*

Introduction   *13*

PART I

Going Back to Cali   *17*

Junebug   *20*

Oceanside, California   *23*

Growing Up Fast   *32*

Flip Phones and Ringback Tones   *37*

Norman, Oklahoma   *45*

Dream Chaser   *58*

Glenn Foster   *69*

PART II

Learning to Be a Pro   *77*

Awakening   *82*

The Night Before   *87*

September 11, 2016   *90*

The Work Begins   *97*

Solidarity   *103*

The Players Coalition   *113*

Boots on the Ground   *123*

Passion, Pain, and Demon Slayin'   *133*

Neuroplasticity   *137*

I Don't Have Time For . . .   *145*

Therapy 149

Still Growing Summit 155

Girls, Girls, Girls, Girls 165

PART III

Brian Flores and Stephen Ross 171

H-Town 181

Habibi Things 186

Breonna Taylor 190

PART IV

Attacking My Fears 203

I Get Out 208

Athletes for Ceasefire 216

Embracing Change 220

Tío Gopher: A Legacy of Pride,
    Resistance, and Reflection 230

Psychedelics and Other Mind-Altering Substances 235

PART V

Tying Up Loose Ends 251

Reflection 253

What's Going on Now 257

Acknowledgments 263

Do the best you can until you know better.
Then when you know better, do better.
—MAYA ANGELOU

I want to take a moment to send my deepest love to everyone who has shown support on this journey, especially when I was in the fire. I've held on to every message, gesture, and act of love. I'm overwhelmed with gratitude; words hardly seem enough to express how much your support has meant to me. It's been my encouragement and my reminder that I am not alone. Thank you, with my whole heart.

I want to say thank you to all of those who have contributed to my life up until this point and in the future. It is already written.

To the women and men who helped shape me into the person I am—the incredible people who gave and expected nothing in return—I am because of you and I serve with your spirit in mind.

To the individuals who did everything possible to hinder my success and well-being, I thank you as well. You can't change what GOD has already written.

Finally, I want to say there are no hard feelings. H*te has no place in my heart and I'm not carrying any grudges. I have peace knowing my truth is out there and each of us has to live with the choices we've made.

With that, I thank you for giving this a read and look forward to working alongside you to leave this place better than we found it.

—*KLDS*

PREFACE
Soul Rebel

WHEN I TOOK A KNEE IN PROTEST of racism and police violence, it was books that opened my eyes to our history and fueled my determination to keep moving forward. That was the driving force behind this project. I wanted those who were curious to hear, directly from me, what was on my mind and what I was experiencing in those moments. Too often, movements are silenced by mass media, with the narrative controlled by those in power, and this one was no exception.

Inside, you'll find everything I remember about the kneeling movement, backed by the receipts. This is my interpretation, no filters, no middlemen. Yes, some memories have faded and certain moments might be left out, but these are the ones that left a lasting impression.

When I look back, one trait stands out: a rebellious streak and a natural resistance to authority. Since my earliest memories, I've been one to test boundaries, challenging rules to see what I could get away with, convinced that common sense should always win over blind obedience. This mindset led to plenty of friction—at home, in school, and eventually in my professional life. But I believe that this habit of pushing back, of standing firm in what feels right, prepared me for the alienation and disapproval I would face later on.

That resistance to just going along with the crowd is what led me to take a knee during the national anthem, a decision that many disagreed with at the time. But just as I had in the past, I stood firm, continuing to protest from September 11, 2016, all the way through my final year with the New Orleans Saints in 2021.

I want to be clear: this is not an autobiography.

My hope is that this book inspires others to discover their innate abilities and use them to make a positive impact on the world. For me, that meant channeling my stubborn nature into something meaningful.

I believe we all have something within us that comes naturally, something we can use to serve the greater good.

In my years as a professional football player, I found my path. I saw a problem and felt called to be part of the solution. I'd prayed for God to use me as part of the plan—expressing that I was willing, and hoping I was ready. Never in my wildest dreams did I imagine stepping onto a political stage, but there I was. Prayer answered.

This book is dedicated to the protest and the personal growth that came through it.

INTRODUCTION

*Your heart has to be able to handle
the weight of your calling.*
—BELL HOOKS

I STOOD ON THE SIDELINE, my heart pounding as the first notes of the national anthem echoed through the stadium. September 11, 2016, a day now etched in American memory, about to become a pivotal moment in my life. As the crowd rose to their feet, I took a deep breath and lowered myself to one knee. In that instant, I joined a growing movement of professional athletes using our platform to protest racial injustice and police brutality. The decision to kneel hadn't come lightly. Raised in a family with military ties and having experienced little overt racism myself, I was an unlikely face of protest. Yet the string of police shootings of unarmed Black men and women across the country had stirred something deep within me.

As the anthem played on, I couldn't have imagined the journey ahead—the history I'd learn, the criticism I'd face, the relationships I'd test, and the lives I'd touch. This was just the beginning of my story, a story that would take me far beyond the football field and into the heart of America's ongoing struggle for equality and justice.

Over the course of this book, I'll give you various insights into my life: my upbringing, my experiences, what led me to activism. And how all of that led me to therapy and the mental health space.

To understand who I am, let's go back to the beginning and let me bring you up to speed.

Part I

GOING BACK TO CALI

I WAS BORN ON APRIL 22, 1992, in Edina, Minnesota. Son of Annette de la O and Kenneth Stills Sr. My mom was a bartender and my father a retired NFL player. I was the fifth and final child for my mother and the second of my father's children. On Mom's side there are three girls and two boys. There's my eldest sister, Natasha; the twins, India and Illiana; my brother, Lance; and then me. The girls have their dad, my brother has his, and I have mine. On my dad's side there's my older sister Clare and my two younger brothers, Lawson and PJ. Clare has her mom, Lawson and PJ have theirs.

Annette and Senior were together on and off during my entire upbringing, but I would say my mother raised me. The earliest memory I have was when I was three, when all my mom's kids and my parents lived in a house together in Milwaukee, Wisconsin. When that didn't work out, Mom and the kids moved back to Minnesota and lived in St. Paul with my grandma. 285 East Wyoming Street. The memories linger of playing sports with my brother and cousins in the front yard. Climbing the huge oak tree near the street and doing everything possible to avoid going into the creepy next-door neighbors' yard.

Grandma's was a two-bedroom multistory home that had a basement and TV room with a pullout couch that we made into a third bedroom. One of my earliest memories of Grandma was going to fetch her a beer and a frozen mug. Then learning the proper way to pour so there wasn't a bunch of foam. The Midwest had loud and rumbling thunderstorms, and there was a Dairy Queen we frequently visited. I loved a banana milkshake, Mom loved the Buster Bar.

I remember going down to the Super America gas station with my brother to get a bag of ninety-nine-cent Hot Cheetos, but my favorite place to eat was an Asian restaurant by the name of Cora's. I loved the spicy fried chicken, fried rice, and cream cheese wontons. Still a must to pick up whenever I visit Minnesota.

When I was five, Annette relocated us to California. Somehow the girls brokered a deal to stay with Grandma to finish high school, leaving Lance and myself making the trip west with Annette and Senior in a U-Haul.

We settled in an apartment complex in the valley of Oceanside, California, my dad's hometown, just outside of Camp Pendleton's military base. My grandpa served in the marines and had a home on Michael Street a couple blocks from the back gate and just around the corner from our new place.

I recall little of our first move to Oceanside. There are memories of our apartment being robbed a handful of times. Then of me flipping over my bicycle handlebars on Valentine's Day and getting stitches over my eyebrow. But soon, we moved back to live with Grandma. I'm guessing making that change was harder than Mom thought, and her being on and off with Senior didn't help.

When we returned to St. Paul, I went to a Catholic school, St. Michael's, which was walking distance from Grandma's. I did not enjoy mass—going from sitting to kneeling to standing and humming strange phrases I didn't understand. I didn't like the uniforms and my teacher smacking my hand with a ruler whenever I was "out of line."

In Minnesota, the winters brought freezing temperatures. We had to bundle up for school and I recall being dared to stick my tongue to a frozen pole, like in *A Christmas Story*. I remember the first time I ate shit on a snowboard—a dare from my cousins to send it straight down the hill without knowing how to stop. And watching MTV with my older sisters. The release of the "Baby One More Time" video with Britney Spears is still etched in my brain. We'd watch *MTV Spring Break*, *Road Rules*, and occasionally a telenovela with Grams.

What I'll never forget is our tradition on Christmas Eve. We'd pack every member of the family in Grandma's home. Tío Gilbert would dress up like Santa Claus and we would sit on his lap and take pictures. And we always had to sing "The Twelve Days of Christmas." We all got to open one gift that evening. That was the moment the kids were waiting for.

JUNEBUG

I was a terror since the public school era.
—CHRISTOPHER WALLACE

MY FAMILY TELLS THIS STORY about a time we were out to lunch and I was acting up. Apparently, I wasn't getting my way so I was crying and lashing out. To that behavior, Grandma asked, "When are you going to stop being a torch?" (Her word for brat.) To which I screamed back, "NEVER!"

The first time I remember breaking the law was when I was six—I stole from a RadioShack. There was only one person working in the store and my mom was keeping his attention occupied at the cash register. I had my eyes on this handheld pinball machine. I had asked for it and she said no. It was winter, so I was wearing a puffy Denver Broncos Starter jacket (Terrell Davis was my favorite player, so they were my favorite team). I took a couple of looks around, then worked up the courage to stuff the machine in my jacket and walk right out. Crazy thing is . . . I got away with it.

My sisters were sitting outside the store when I joined them and shared what I had done. When Mom came out, they told on me. The next day, we returned to the store, and the manager warned me that if I ever did that again, he would call the police and have me taken to jail. I don't remember being afraid of the police, but I was terrified of what my dad would say. He was thousands of miles away, yet I cried, anxious about what would happen to me.

Over the years, my rebellious nature would evolve. I struggled with authority. One of those kids who did the opposite of what I was told. If there was a rule, I was going to bend or break it. I ate on the school bus when there was a clear *No Eating or Drinking* sign. I made alterations to school and sports uniforms. I stole and lied to see what I could get away with. Rules didn't apply unless I got caught.

I was a curious child, always seeking explanations for everything, but my upbringing didn't encourage that kind of questioning. My parents often responded with, "Because I said so," which never satisfied me.

As the years went by, I found different ways to express myself. I started getting tattoos at sixteen, fully aware that one day I would cover my entire body. Even at a young age, I recognized the negative stigma surrounding tattoos and wanted to challenge it. I believe tattoos are a form of art and self-expression.

My next big jump would be into mind-altering substances. In my youth, I huffed air freshener, smoked weed, did Ecstasy and psychedelic mushrooms. All in the interest of exploration. I didn't subscribe to the rules of society and wasn't worried about the laws. I don't recall ever feeling guilty or worrying about what anybody thought about me exploring, either.

In college, inspired by Wiz Khalifa, I decided to dye my hair. He was on the cover of *Rolling Stone* with a little patch of blond in the front of his 'fro. I thought it was fly but didn't want to completely bite his style, so I grew a mohawk and bleached the back half. That's when the "Pony" was born. A name given to me by my boy Mike Hodges, who would end up becoming my stylist in later years.

I was a broke college kid, so I asked a girl friend to do an at-home bleach. We bought a kit from the store and got to it in the bathroom tub. Naturally, the first attempt at taking dark hair to light turned out horribly. The back of my head was dark orange, definitely not ready for public viewing. Still, with classes, team meetings, and practice, it was going to be seen. The first team meeting post-bleach, I said, *Fuck it, bring on the jokes—no hat or hood, let's see what they have to say.* The jokes flowed freely and I took them on the chin. I even recall being told by staff that I would "never be the face of the program looking like that."

For some reason, the negativity only fueled my desire to keep it. I knew we needed to get the tone right, but I wanted to stick to my idea. It wasn't very long before kids all around the US copied that style. My hair even has its own Twitter account, @KennyStillsHair (not created or run by me).

OCEANSIDE, CALIFORNIA

Ain't a hood n*gga but a n*gga from the hood.
See, Mama stayed on me so I turned out pretty good.
—ANDRÉ 3000

IN 1999, WE MOVED BACK TO OCEANSIDE just in time for me to enroll in second grade. My parents were together for a year or so before we'd relocate back to St. Paul for the last time. From kindergarten to high school, I'd attend seven different schools all over North County (San Diego) and in Minnesota. Throughout that time, my parents were on and off and even went through a custody battle. A remorseful core memory I have is being forced to choose between the two.

In the bathroom of a Chili's, my dad got down on my level and asked who I wanted to live with. I remember feeling torn between not wanting to leave Mom alone by choosing Dad, and not wanting to hurt Dad's feelings by choosing Mom. I also recall us being "on the run," trying to avoid being served with papers, and eventually Mom having to attend court.

Things began to get stable when Mom started managing apartment complexes. Having her as the manager meant we had a place to live, so we didn't need to worry about a roof over our heads. One place she managed was in the valley of Oceanside, close to my grandpa's old house. I never felt unsafe but there were rival gangs within a couple blocks of each other. And members of said gangs living in our apartment building.

Because of sports, I didn't get pulled into gang life, though the "hood mentality" was still a part of me. I know it might sound cliché, like I'm trying to fit into some tough-guy narrative, but it's important for you to understand where I come from. Growing up, the environment around me reinforced certain stereotypes: the struggle, suppressed emotions, self-reliance, and an attitude built on survival and street smarts.

Even though I wasn't gang-affiliated, I still had to follow the unspoken rules of the streets. We were all labeled the same, whether we belonged or not. I knew I wasn't a part of that life, but the influence still seeped in. I had to learn how to read the room, when to stand my ground, and how to move through a world where respect, toughness, and loyalty meant everything. The people around me, the neighborhood, those unwritten codes—they all shaped how I thought, how I moved, and how I saw the world. And even now, those lessons are with me.

Oceanside is a tough town with a strong military presence. If you were to ride down the coast nowadays, you might not know this. Over the past ten years, there's been a process of gentrification. New buildings, cleaner streets, craft breweries, white women in yoga outfits.

When I was growing up, it wasn't like that. It was common for people to be stabbed or shot down by the beach—gang violence or even drunken marine violence. Pick your poison.

And if things weren't poppin' off by the beach, they were in the valley.

The two gangs in my neighborhood were the Deep Valley Bloods and the Deep Valley Crips. During my time in the valley, there was a spree of murders and retaliations. When I was thirteen, Rusty Seau (cousin to the legendary late linebacker Junior) was shot and killed. Rusty was sixteen and lived in our complex. Nineteen days later, another teenager named Joaquin Pruitt was killed in what was rumored to be retaliation.

The gangs were around, but I always steered clear. I knew the rules: don't wear their colors, don't start any trouble, don't mess with their women, keep your head down when they're around, and if things go sideways, RUN. I became a master in street smarts— cool on the outside but always on edge and anticipating the unexpected. I had to learn how to move, how to avoid trouble, and how to read a situation before it escalated.

Oceanside runs four miles along the coast and then stretches twenty miles inland toward the 15 freeway; the 5 is the coastal freeway and the 15 the inland. On any given day, it can take thirty to forty-five minutes to get from one to the other, using the side streets. And maybe twenty-five if you take the connecting 76 freeway. I grew up as far inland as you could be in Oceanside. And if you head north, you'll reach Fallbrook, our neighboring town to the east.

The only time we visited that place was to play

sports. Growing up, stories were told of crosses burning back there. Come to find out one of the most notorious white supremacists lived in Fallbrook: Tom Metzger, who passed in November 2020.

Through my youth in Oceanside, I played football, baseball, basketball, and ran track. Most, if not all, of my coaches and the parents had military ties or served at some point themselves. We were taught hard work and discipline as the foundation of everything we did. We were supposed to be tough, fearless, and respectful of everyone we came across. All the kids I knew got some form of physical punishment and it kept us all in line. But this also reinforced violence as part of our masculinity, something I'd have to address later in life.

My best friend in Oceanside was Joe Mascarenaz, aka Little Joe or Joe Joe. With birth dates only a month and a day apart, Joe and I were inseparable. We played sports together from elementary school up until high school. I spent most weekends at his house. We played *NCAA Football* and watched the Friday movies series until we knew every word by heart. On our football team, his parents, Joe and Diana, were our head coach and team mom. But they were more than that to me. They were my second family, and to this day I still feel that way. They have always treated me like one of their own and have asked for nothing but respect and love in return.

My all-time favorite sports memory is from Oceanside Pop Warner. When I was ten years old, our team, the Oceanside Mighty Pirates, went undefeated and earned an invite to the Pop Warner Super Bowl in Orlando, Florida. After doing everything needed to raise the money, we made our way across the country to the Disney sports complex. In true marine fashion, our team wore matching windbreakers and walked everywhere in two silent lines, whether at the airport, on the bus, or around Disney. But I wasn't having it. I fought back against the uniformity, wearing my hat backward or pulling up one pant leg. I refused to blend in, determined not to be like everyone else. Even so, Disney wrote a letter afterward stating that we were the most well-behaved team they had ever hosted.

I remember our first night at the Disney sports complex like it was yesterday. We had traveled all day and got checked into our rooms late. Four kids per room with a joined door left open in between. After we were tucked in, we were instructed to go right to sleep. They let us know that one of the coaches or team moms would be patrolling the halls and to be on our best behavior. The front door to our room was left cracked open just in case. But we were full of too much excitement; one thing led to another and both rooms ended up having a massive pillow fight. Laughing and screaming, we were eventually caught. The next morning the team got a talking-to. If that were to happen again, the whole team would lose our privileges at Disney.

On that trip we faced a team from Raleigh, North Carolina, and a team from Providence, Rhode Island. Beating both of them to be crowned the CHAMPS.

In our first game, I took the opening kickoff to the house to set the tone.

Winning that championship has always stayed with me. Playing for Coach Joe instilled a strong work ethic in us. He emphasized toughness and discipline and ran us just like the marines. We did enough up-downs, six-inch holds, and bear crawls to last a lifetime. That year, we dominated almost every team we faced. In fact, when a team finally scored against us late in the season, one of our players cried in anger.

Maybe I remember that season so vividly because of the bonds I formed with my teammates, or because we essentially got to go on a family trip to Disney. Perhaps it was because my dad was there in Florida with us, when he usually missed my games due to his own coaching jobs. Whatever the reason, I know it was the first time I truly understood what hard work and dedication could achieve.

That trip gave us unforgettable memories and extreme confidence. The group of kids I played with would go on to win multiple state championships and section titles at Oceanside High.

My coaches were my mentors. Men who poured into me on and off the field. When Mom couldn't get through to me, she'd rely on them to deliver the message. These families fed me and let me stay at their houses. They'd go out of their way to pick me up and make sure I made it to practice. Some families even helped sponsor me when we couldn't afford to cover costs.

The anti-military narrative that was later created around taking a knee during the national anthem couldn't be further from the truth. I wouldn't be where I am without the sacrifices of service members here and abroad, and I hold that deeply in my heart. My choice to kneel wasn't a rejection of their service, it was an effort to honor the ideals they protect. I was embodying the true spirit of American values: standing up for freedom, justice, and equality. The promises our country makes to all its people.

Over the years, I've wrestled with my feelings about the military. Growing up in Oceanside, we were raised to be patriotic, to honor those who serve, and to respect their dedication and sacrifice. And I still do. The courage, discipline, and selflessness of the individuals who put their lives on the line are undeniable. But as I got older, I found myself asking deeper questions. Not about the people in uniform, but about the systems that command them.

I started to realize that while many serve with the noblest of intentions, the larger forces at play don't always embrace those same values. There's a stark difference between defending one's country and waging wars that, beneath the surface, are driven more by profit than by true national security. And that's where things get complicated.

I can fully support the idea of protecting the US and its allies, but it's harder to accept that war, something that costs so many lives, can also be a business. Private defense contractors make billions of dollars off prolonged conflicts, sometimes with little regard for the well-being of soldiers or civilians. That reality sits uneasily with the values we claim to uphold.

Take the Iraq War in 2003. We were told it was necessary to protect the world from weapons of mass destruction. But when those weapons were never found, the war didn't stop. It continued for years, leading to enormous loss of life and economic devastation. All the while, certain defense companies saw record profits. This wasn't an isolated event; history is full of examples where the interests of a few have outweighed the sacrifices of many.

These realities force us to ask hard questions. If we truly respect our troops, shouldn't we also demand that their lives not be risked for wars built on misinformation or financial gain? If we value peace, shouldn't we invest as much in diplomacy and global cooperation as we do in military force?

I know the world is complex. Conflict has existed for as long as humanity itself, and achieving world peace may always seem out of reach. But that doesn't mean we shouldn't push for a better way. If we continue down this path where unchecked greed fuels war and global tensions escalate without accountability, we are setting ourselves up for destruction.

I don't pretend to have all the answers. But I do know this: respecting the military means more than just honoring service; it means questioning the decisions that put service members in harm's way. It means striving for a world where war is a last resort, not a business model. The pursuit of peace is difficult, but it's necessary. And if humanity has any hope of survival, we have to start walking that path together.

GROWING UP FAST

By age twelve, it was just Mom and me. Lance was sent back to Minnesota to live with his father as he was becoming too much for Mom to handle. It was around then that I started coming into my own. Sixth grade began my "pretty boy" era. The gap between my two front teeth grew together, my big lips started to fit my face, and girls began to notice me. An attention I couldn't resist. Having good hygiene, moisturizing my skin, and how I dressed all of a sudden mattered.

I used to rock Phat Farm and G-Unit gear, all from Burlington Coat Factory. But my core outfits? They were all about creased Dickies shorts, loose denim jeans, and layered "tall Ts" (at least three of 'em). I'd throw on Vans, Chucks, or Adidas shell toes, with layered socks, one black over the white. I even stuffed socks into my shoes to make the tongues pop out, and wrapped rubber bands around the bottoms of my jeans so they wouldn't drag on the ground. The colors? Black, white, or gray, since we weren't allowed to wear any solid colors at school.

It was around then that I started becoming interested in weed. I bought my first dime bag between periods in the sixth grade. I suspect one of my classmates reported me for having it because the next thing I knew, the assistant principal was in our class asking me to step outside with my backpack. I quickly tucked the tree into the coin pocket of my jeans and tried to act calm. They searched my bags and patted me down but couldn't find the bud. Eventually, they let me go. I returned to class smirking, looking around to figure out who the snitch was. That was the first time I escaped trouble, but it wouldn't be the last.

My mom would eventually find that same dime bag hidden in the bottom of my Nintendo Game-Cube. I guess the bud reeked. I lied to her and said I was holding it for a friend. She doubted I was telling the truth and threatened to drug-test me. Which would've been fine since I wasn't actually smoking. I guess it just felt cool to have it in my possession. When I convinced a friend to say it was his, she finally got off my case. Lying was another behavior I'd have to learn to shake.

At the same time, my dad was overseas coaching in the NFL Europe. Because of that, I got to visit Barcelona, Spain and Frankfurt, Germany. I didn't know it then but those visits normalized international travel for me. They helped with my comfort and sparked more curiosity for exploration.

We'd get a call from Senior here and there, but the daily male influence was coming from my coaches and friends' parents. They saw my potential and didn't want it to go to waste. They'd pull me aside from time to time, trying to instill their wisdom. I'd listen attentively and feel like what they were saying made sense. "Take care of your school work, listen to your mother, stay away from the wrong crowds." All the advice and reminders I needed. I did what I needed to pass in school, I reluctantly listened to my mom, and I didn't feel like the crowd I hung out with was an issue.

One of those conversations really stuck with me. I had a coach who was moved to tears with passion and concern. He mentioned the talented kids from the neighborhood who lost focus and fell off. And made me promise not to be one of those guys. I made the promise and often thought about that conversation.

Looking back, I see why everyone was so uptight— one wrong decision could affect everything. Wrong place at the wrong time and our lives can change completely. Though everyone else was concerned, I thought I had it all figured out.

As I started to come into my teens, Mom was on high alert. She'd found weed in the house again, I had a "serious" girlfriend, and the pattern of kids having kids in my family was common. She'd started when she was eighteen, Tasha the same, and Illiana not long thereafter. Mom was doing everything she could to protect me and I was doing everything I could to break out.

The parents of most of the kids I hung out with in my "pretty boy" era were a lot more lenient than Coach Joe and Ms. Diana. At their house, it was school, church, and sports. We weren't allowed to be out all night, online at all hours, or on the phone talking to girls. We were watched like a hawk and expected to act accordingly. Outside of their home, I had the freedom I yearned for. I thought I was grown and the universe wasn't telling me otherwise.

I wanted more independence and although I got it, my life was rarely in danger and I stayed away from teenage pregnancy. I like to think that either Annette raised me well or I simply got lucky. It was probably a combination of both.

The summer before my freshman year of high school, I got arrested. I know, you're probably saying to yourself, *I thought you had it all figured out*, but it was one of those wrong place, wrong time situations.

We were at the local movie theater and two kids I knew were about to fight. Of course, we followed with anticipation. The two squared up but nothing happened, both waiting on the other to throw the first punch. When they went their separate ways, one boy pounded a car in frustration. The owner of said car saw this happen and called the police. When the police arrived, they put all of us in handcuffs as accomplices to the crime. The officers then told us to call our parents. If someone answered and could come and get us, they'd let us go. If not, they'd have to take us in. Luckily, Annette answered and I was free to go.

Before I knew it, my high school plans were up in the air. I dreamed of going to Oceanside High, where all my childhood friends would be, but my parents had a different vision. The sight of me in handcuffs solidified their fears and pushed them to move me away from the O. Mom saw too many similarities to the neighborhood she grew up in on the west side of St. Paul, Minnesota, and she was determined to offer me a different path. Her biggest worries were gangs, drugs, and teen pregnancies.

With those concerns in mind, she enrolled me at La Costa Canyon High School, about thirty minutes south. At the time, it felt less like a wise decision and more like a punishment. Little did I know, this change would set me on a course that would completely re-shape my life.

FLIP PHONES AND RINGBACK TONES

Hard work beats talent when talent doesn't work hard.

THE DECISION TO MOVE TO ENCINITAS stands out as one of the most significant choices my parents ever made. I didn't talk to my mom for what felt like months. According to her, it was only a couple weeks. I sat at the dinner table in silence to protest the move. Oceanside was a football powerhouse, currently boasting sixteen section championships and two state titles. (The boys I grew up with won four section titles and the first state title in school history.) We knew the talent we had and the tradition of the school. And after most of our Little League team had agreed to play together, I was excited to finally be attending school with my teammates. These boys were and still are my brothers; after all, we'd been playing together since we were seven years old. I was beyond frustrated to be moved and couldn't comprehend the decision.

La Costa Canyon High (LCC) is located in Carlsbad, California, a super laid-back town known for its exceptional quality of life, beautiful beaches, and eclectic vibe. The school is located about twenty minutes inland from the beach, in between the hills. The year that I enrolled would be only its eighth in existence.

The story of Black athletes seeking better education and opportunities in affluent neighborhoods is all too familiar. Across the US, Black and Brown students are often recruited and bused to private schools. In my case, La Costa Canyon was a public school, and I wasn't being actively recruited. Yet I couldn't shake the feeling of being like one of those kids in the movies, leaving my roots behind in search of something more.

I now see why my parents made that decision. We are shaped by our environment, and the odds were already stacked against me. I hadn't shown the maturity to navigate those challenges, so they decided to take action for my future.

This was my first time seeing whites as the majority . . . a considerable culture shock. Oceanside felt like the "melting pot" we were taught America is supposed to be. Encinitas was more of a white picket fence, golden lab, all-American-dream type of place. We had surfing as an elective and were ranked nationally in lacrosse. I'd never even heard of lacrosse. There were maybe five Black kids in the entire school, and only one Black teacher. I felt terribly out of place; everyone knew about the new Black kid at school. The thing I was lucky to have was sports, one of the greatest human connectors.

It was summer football workouts, and Mom would drop me off for a couple of hours of training. Afterward, I had the choice to either walk an hour and a half home or wait for her to pick me up during her lunch break. One afternoon, a group of the guys approached and invited me to hang. With nothing else on my agenda, I gladly joined them. We walked down the canyon and up the street to one of their houses.

Having mostly lived in apartments, I was in awe of what I saw. This house wasn't just a home, it was a whole new world. There was a housekeeper, a granny flat, an intercom system in every room that connected to the kitchen, three fully stocked fridges, a pool with a slide, and a walk-in pantry loaded with every snack a growing boy could dream of. I had never seen anything like it. Suddenly, my aspirations grew bigger.

At first I fought the change, desperately trying to return to Oceanside on the weekends. But over time, something began to shift. I started seeing the benefits of this new life. In my old neighborhood, freedom often came with real risks, and the price of that freedom was too high. But here, I felt a sense of safety and stability I'd never experienced before. An environment where the expectation wasn't just to go to college, but to attend one of the *best* colleges. It was a place where kids weren't defined by their backgrounds or limited by stereotypes.

It was here that I realized the full potential of my skills, and what they could mean for my family's future. I began to imagine a life for us in a beautiful, spacious home, in a quiet, friendly neighborhood. I saw a new vision for myself, not just as a kid from the hood, but as someone who could defy expectations, break through the stereotypes, and create a life beyond what anyone thought was possible. For the first time, I saw a clear path forward—not just for me, but for the life I wanted to build for my family.

What really made this place stand out were the parents. I found myself surrounded by families who seemed to embody values and character, people who had worked hard for everything they had. Most of them were middle to upper class, but what struck me wasn't just their financial success, it was how the kids interacted with their parents. There was none of that spoiled, back-talking, temper-tantrum behavior you see on TV. Instead, these kids genuinely respected their parents. Not only were they well-behaved, they understood the importance of hard work, respect, and responsibility.

I had a smart and sporty group of friends; they were athletic but also worked hard at their crafts. Where I'd come from, guys got by on athleticism. Not to say that we didn't work hard, but as we got older it wasn't "cool" to try hard or do extra. The boys in La Costa were always doing extra—that's how they kept up and why they excelled. I'd grown up playing against these annoying "try hard" white boys, and now that characteristic was rubbing off on me. By combining that attitude with my talent, I was able to elevate my game to a whole new level.

The move was a tough transition for us. Anyone who's tried to move up in the socioeconomic world knows the challenges it brings. It caused some friction with the parents from our old neighborhood; some even thought we were acting like we were "better than," which wasn't the case at all.

Ultimately, every place has its struggles, and LCC had its own set of problems, just not the ones Mom was concerned about. What I did find, though, was a group of friends who were competitive, strong-willed, and ambitious. We were tight-knit, always playing organized sports or setting up our own games—hoops, Wiffle ball, beach volleyball. We were constantly active, pushing each other. We didn't feel the weight of the world outside as much, and in that bubble, there was a clear, unspoken expectation: to succeed and to prosper. Looking back, that was the real shift for me, the understanding that being in an environment where high expectations were the norm made me start to raise my own bar.

On one of my hands, I have a tattoo of a compass. It symbolizes my ability to navigate life without relying on parental guidance. Over the years, I found families I looked up to and I made sure to spend time with them. I've befriended random people I've met online and even went on a snowboard trip with a family I met at an autograph signing. I've trusted my gut when reading people's energy and somehow I've managed to stay safe, failed to be seriously taken advantage of, and have built a beautiful tribe of family that isn't blood-related.

I knew from a young age to surround myself with people I wanted to emulate. At my house after dinner, we had to help clean up and do the dishes. I took that with me wherever I went. When I'd get invited to friends' homes for dinner, I'd scarf down whatever they served and then stay around to help clean. The other kids would head out but I wanted to hang around the parents. Getting to know them, asking questions, soaking up as much knowledge as possible. Those moments interacting with other families set the stage for what I could see for myself in the future. I valued that time. And to this day, I love a long chat with the elders in my life. Figuring out how to find adults to confide in and learn from had immense value. I was beginning to understand that different people could play different roles in my life. Whatever I couldn't get from my own parents, I could find somewhere else.

In my teens, racial epithets and homophobia were pretty normalized. *Gay, faggot, no homo*, and *pause* were overused. Asians were *chinks*, *Indians* meant Native Americans AND people from India. Or were they the same? Pure ignorance. Kids in Encinitas knew better than to say the N-word or wear blackface, but the microaggressions still existed. It was assumed that I couldn't swim, I'd heard a boombox be referred to as a *ghetto blaster,* and I'd been told that I spoke well for a Black guy. All stereotypical BS.

On campus, there were two main areas where people hung out during lunch. In the quad, there were windows where you could buy a pan pizza, Caesar salad, water, Gatorade, and baked chips. The other area was shaded and where those of us who got free lunch would go. I qualified but rarely ate it as the food was disgusting. That was mainly where our

Latino students hung. The school was segregated in this way but I never heard any flagrant, hateful discussion. Most of the school hung out in the quad, the Latinos hung out down by the "free lunch" counter, everybody else dispersed around campus, and the seniors ate off campus.

I ate in the quad; Mom would make PB&J sandwiches with Hot Cheetos or a huge breakfast burrito. And friends would occasionally spot me.

I grew up believing that we had moved past racism and that Black people now had equal rights. While I never noticed overt racism in school, everything changed later, after I took a knee.

The fun most kids start to have in college, we had in high school. Not every parent was on board, but the general consensus was to prioritize safety and responsibility when it came to partying. Some parents even allowed us to drink under their supervision. Since we were going to do it anyway, having an adult around felt like the safer choice. Because of this, my close group of friends navigated high school without any major loss or tragedy, and for that I'm truly grateful.

It might sound strange to say we handled our partying responsibly at that age, but we truly did. Beer pong, dizzy bat—name any drinking game, I'll take my crew over yours.

One year, we made a trip to Stanford to visit a friend's sister, explore the campus, and catch a football game. Naturally, we kicked things off with a pregame, and soon enough we found ourselves facing off against some students at the beer pong table.

We were confident but slightly out of our element—being that everyone had different house rules. We quickly adapted and ended up leaving undefeated, talking shit the whole way, even skunking a couple of guys and making them sit under the table until the next game was over. Those were the days: all fun and minimal responsibilities.

Back at school, we'd sit in the parking lot after practice and shoot the shit, some guys "sapping a brew" or throwing a dip or both. We'd get fried every Thursday night before our team dinners, giggling uncontrollably and demolishing whatever food the parents served us. Life was GEWD! House parties, party buses, teen clubs—there was little that my high school experience didn't prepare me for.

NORMAN, OKLAHOMA

Arriving in Norman, Oklahoma on a full athletic scholarship in the winter of 2009 was another culture shock. Luckily, I made the commitment with fellow San Diegans Tony Jefferson and Brennan Clay. Tony and I both graduated early in order to give ourselves the best chance to start as freshmen. Enrolling early gives the student athlete an opportunity to get a jump on the college experience: classes, workouts, practice . . . socializing. I had fully moved into the dorms and was ready to get into the swing of things when I received the news that the NCAA was not going to accept a few of my high school credits. Reluctantly, I had to head back to San Diego and take three more classes in order to be eligible. Luckily, LCC had a class where students could do school at their own pace. You got the textbook and worksheets for each chapter. When you finished the book and passed the test, you got the credit. I knocked that out quickly and was right back to Norman.

We never really considered the biting-cold winds and occasional snowstorms that winters in Oklahoma would bring. When I'd visited in the fall, it was chilly, but for some reason I thought it wouldn't dip below freezing in "the South." I was definitely wrong. Waking up for those early five thirty a.m. workouts was torture. The training was tough enough, but getting up at the crack of dawn while adjusting to the frigid weather added a whole new layer.

Some mornings, I'd wake up and yell to Tony in the other room: "You going today?" His reply of "Hell nah!" was all the encouragement I needed to stay in bed. We missed a few workouts early on, and that meant facing Smitty—Jerry Schmidt, our strength coach. He was a stout man with a no-nonsense attitude; we spent more time with him than with our actual coaches.

All things disciplinary ran through Smitty, and if we got injured, our lives became a living hell. The thought was to work us so hard, we'd rather practice than be injured, and boy did that work. Here's when we learned the difference between being injured and being *hurt*.

His punishment usually started with a stern talking-to, where he'd turn his back to us, exclaiming, "I thought we already talked about this, big dog!" He'd follow up with, "How are we gonna win the Big 12 if we don't put in the work?" All the while making it clear he didn't want to hear any excuses. All he wanted to see was . . . WORK. Smitty had a way of making us feel terrible for letting him and the team down—and our punishment? Thirty minutes on the StairMaster at level twelve.

Eventually, we managed to get our act together, but that transition was definitely a challenge. At one point, Tony even considered transferring. I often found myself lying awake at night, anxious about what the training would bring the next morning. The fear of oversleeping and being late loomed large in my mind. Missing a workout meant facing the dreaded StairMaster, then completing the workout later.

Working with Smitty and the strength staff showed us what we were capable of. They pushed the body further than the mind thought was possible. Breaking us mentally and physically, then helping to put us back together. A monumental experience in my life.

After a winter, spring, and summer in Norman, I felt like a Spartan in the movie *300*. I was now fifteen pounds heavier and number two on the depth chart.

My freshman year, we had an impressive season, winning our conference and the Fiesta Bowl. I was a starter for every game and scored my first touchdown in week five against our rival, Texas. I quickly adapted to college life, opting for a major in communication, even though I had no clear idea of what I wanted to pursue outside of football—my focus was entirely on the game.

The only thing my mom asked of me was to get my degree. So there I was, balancing my studies and my passion.

Outside of ball, I was being introduced to Boosie, Webbie, Currensy, Gucci Mane, Z-Ro, and all the Southern rappers. We ate Slim Chickens, Raising

Canes, and Braums. I tried fried okra and Oklahoma's version of barbecue. I cherished learning about and connecting with my teammates from all over the country. I felt like I was fitting in seamlessly. The biggest struggle came from dealing with the head ball coach, Bob Stoops.

Coach belonged to the older generation, which held a negative viewpoint on cannabis. He believed pot smokers were "losers," so we were constantly being drug-tested. He went out of his way to remove every player who smoked, not understanding the benefits of the plant medicine. When I wasn't smoking, living in Norman was bleak, my body hurt, and the stress made me irritable. When I *was* smoking, all my worries went out the window, besides the thought of when I'd be drug-tested again.

Through my time in school, I was on and off cannabis, but because of the testing, I tried synthetic weed and drank excessively to cope. For a period of time, I took Xanax and drank to fully black myself out. I was going to escape one way or another. You might ask, *Escape what?*

I think the pressure of my position, combined with my dreams and aspirations, weighed heavily on me. Lacking emotional maturity, my only outlet was sports, and each day felt like a battle, mentally and physically. Football was a year-round commitment, and on top of that, I had school to manage.

Mornings began with intense workouts before class, and then I'd rush to avoid being late or marked absent. In class, I struggled to stay awake after pushing myself to the limit during workouts. After classes, there were meetings followed by practice, and then it was time for recovery and homework, only to wake up and do it all over again. It felt like Navy SEAL training, and I desperately needed a way to release some of that built-up tension.

For me, cannabis provided that escape. It brought me a sense of peace and happiness, allowing me to unwind from the relentless pressure. I've always believed that because my coping mechanism was natural and didn't hurt others, I wasn't doing anything wrong. If I could handle my schoolwork and play well on the field, why was it such a big deal?

Not only were we stressed, but I also had a nagging feeling that we were being taken advantage of. I saw my jersey in the student store and in the crowd, and I noticed people copying my hairstyle. I felt I should be able to capitalize on that attention. Back then, the rules didn't allow it, but nowadays, students can profit from their name, image, and likeness, and I'm genuinely happy for them.

During my time, scholarship checks were $900 a month, with $600 going to rent and $100 for my phone bill. We had a limited number of meal swipes at our outdated athlete cafeteria, which offered barely edible food. That left us with only $200 for everything else. Occasionally, I'd get a gift card from a friend or we'd go over to the regular student cafeteria and ask to be swiped in.

We were broke but never went hungry. And even though it was against the rules, people looked out for us. I never received any cash directly, but if I was in a crunch I had people I could go to.

One thing I avoided was opening a credit card, something my dad strongly advised against. While it might have been nice to start building my credit, who knows how I would've used that thing in a pinch.

One of the biggest struggles was the rigid system we all had to follow, especially when it came to attending class and mandatory study hall. Young and defiant, I didn't see the issue as long as I was passing my classes. I disagreed with the rules, and that led to my rebellion. I knew I had to attend class to avoid suspension, but I never completed my ten hours of weekly mandatory study hall. I didn't need help with my classes, and being stuck in the tutoring center with other athletes would've been a problem. I understood that if I wasn't challenged and had too much free time, I'd likely cause trouble. So I did what I thought was best: I stayed away. Bob Stoops, however, was not a fan of this behavior.

The person who had to handle my rebellion was my position coach, Jay Norvell, and I certainly gave him a run for his money. My antics often came with punishments that he had to enforce. Waking up at five a.m. on "off days" to watch me barrel roll across the field while talking smack was probably not how he wanted to spend his mornings. With most of us far from home, he became somewhat of a father figure, juggling coaching and recruiting alongside his responsibilities as a husband and father. I appreciated his old-school coaching style and the wisdom he shared, like a story he would tell about "the old bull."

Coach Norvell was also the first person to introduce me to meditation. During training camp meetings, we'd take breaks to lie on the floor and visualize ourselves receiving signals from the sideline, making plays, executing crucial blocks, making big catches, and celebrating with our teammates. While most of the guys used that time to take a nap, I have to give Coach Jay credit for introducing us to a practice that could help us both on and off the field.

Because I enrolled early and we had such a big freshman class, after half a semester in the dorms, I got to move off campus. Coach Jay would come check on us randomly, usually during a weekend after we'd partied and were all hungover. He'd be on us about taking out the trash and cleaning up our spot, typical parent stuff.

On the field, he helped us become technicians. We'd watch old tapes of Marvin Harrison, Torry Holt, and Isaac Bruce—three of the baddest to ever do it— learning to get open, play fast, and get loose with the ball in our hands. Coach knew how to motivate us, keeping track of every statistic and rewarding us for blocks and knockdowns as well as big plays. Outside of my defiant behavior, we got along really well and I'm thankful for our time together. I challenged him on everything from life lessons to the weekly game install, and we had our fair share of battles. But he prepared me for the next level and tried to make me a better young man, and for that I'm forever grateful.

As I've mentioned, during that first year we

clinched the Big 12 Championship and the Fiesta Bowl. (I was also runner-up for Newcomer of the Year.) That early success inflated my ego like a hot-air balloon; I felt untouchable and indestructible. But it didn't take long for reality to knock me back down to earth.

On the first weekend back after our winter break, my heart sank as I saw the flashing lights behind me and was pulled over for driving under the influence. Many won't admit this, but it certainly wasn't my first time drinking and driving. Back then, we didn't have Uber and the local rideshare took upward of an hour.

I vividly remember that night. As I left 747, a local bar, someone recognized me and offered to buy one last shot of tequila. After downing it, I felt a mix of confidence and carelessness. Every person I passed asked if I needed a ride, but I had a little after-party planned with a few teammates and some girls. I figured I could handle the drive just a couple of blocks home.

As I sat in my Ford Crown Victoria, door ajar, a teammate pulled up and urged me to take a ride. I waved him off, convinced I was fine. Some friends piled into my car with me, and as we drove, someone in the backseat lit up a Black & Mild. I wanted a hit, so I turned to reach for it, but as I did, the car veered up onto the curb. A quick correction got us back on track, but little did I know, a cop was lurking behind a nearby house, ready to catch drunk drivers.

He pulled us over and asked me to take a sobriety

test, but then informed me he didn't have a Breathalyzer and I'd need to be taken in.

As I was being arrested, Tony stepped in, talking shit to the cops and insisting he didn't want me to face this alone. So they arrested him too. In hindsight, it was a reckless move on his part, but it spoke volumes about our friendship and I'll never forget it. As a result of the incident, I faced suspension for the first game of the next season. (*Forever indebted to you for that, TJeff, thank you for showing me what true friendship looks like!*)

That experience humbled me in every way possible. I'd embarrassed myself and my family. Seeing my mug shot splashed across the newspaper and on TV made me realize just how quickly things can change. Hero one day and zero the next. The only words of comfort I remember hearing were from Tony. I was very hard on myself and worried about what the outside world thought. Tony affirmed me, letting me know that we all make mistakes and that this too would blow over. The majority of what I received was tough love, and while that usually helped, I know now the importance of grace in times of struggle. It felt like me against the world (and that actually further fueled my determination). The mistake didn't stop me from partying or drinking. Far from it—but it did teach me how swiftly the tides can turn.

That boneheaded decision cost me $10k and my reputation, and it obviously could've been a lot worse. Nowadays there's plenty of rideshare services, please use them.

* * *

In high school, I didn't think much about race relations; our team was predominantly white, and we all hung out together without any issues. However, when I got to the University of Oklahoma (OU), I quickly noticed things were different. There were Black parties and white parties, often separated by music, vibe, or personal preference. Tony was our "in" with the white crowd. As California boys, we were known for being friendly and outgoing, and Tony embodied that spirit. He made friends with the fraternity guys, who started inviting a few of us to their parties. Some of these guys felt the need to protect their territory, having been robbed by other athletes in the past, while others simply didn't want us around.

It wasn't until after we left, in 2015, that I learned the foundation some of the frats were built on. Members of one of OU's prestigious fraternities, Sigma Alpha Epsilon, had videotaped themselves chanting, "*There will never be a nigger SAE. You can hang them from a tree, but they'll never sign with me. There will never be a nigger SAE.*"

At the time, I didn't grasp the dynamics at play in these relationships. For many of us, this begins as early as high school. We find ourselves navigating a landscape where our presence seems to elevate others' status, creating a facade of acceptance. We enjoy the perks—free drinks or a place to party—and they know better than to express prejudiced sentiments in our presence. This reflects a backhanded privilege that Black entertainers often face: everyone wants to befriend us, but how do they behave when we're not around?

Not only were the parties segregated, but so were the locker rooms. While some of that separation is natural due to the positions we play, it has always bothered me. I've made it a point to connect these fractures throughout my career. We even crashed our white teammates' parties occasionally to try to bridge the gap.

In college and the NFL, this pattern continued. White players often ate together in the cafeteria, sat together on the bus, and socialized outside the facility. While there were exceptions, this was the predominant dynamic I observed.

In my three years at OU, we were undefeated against Texas. We won two Big 12 Championships and played in two BCS bowl games. I was never voted captain (by the coaches), but I was one of the team leaders.

Every weekend they'd assign me recruits to host and get to commit. They got on me for being the party boy but knew where to send all the top recruits. So weekly I'd host dudes from high school, junior college (JUCO), and even potential grad transfers. With a pretty high success rate too. I wanted to win a national championship and that always came first, but we also loved to have a good time. I earned this opportunity and wanted to make the most of it.

When it came to my teammates, I did everything I could to make every player feel like family. We had an open-door policy at our home and always hosted guys for holidays, to watch games or just get high and kick it.

I'm biased, but I felt like we had the talent to win a national championship, we just lacked in the coaching department. Losing our defensive coordinator, Brent Venables, to Clemson hurt. As well as our offensive coordinator, Kevin Wilson. We hired in the Stoops family on defense and from within the program on offense. It was here that I started to see how coaching staffs are built. Instead of hiring the best guy, they hire the guy they know and trust. To me, those decisions make all the difference.

After Johnny Manziel and Texas A&M trounced us at the Cotton Bowl during our junior year, Tony and I approached Bob in the hallway of our team hotel to announce our decision to declare for the NFL draft. He looked at us with disgust, saying, "You're making the biggest mistake of your lives," before turning away. Undeterred, I packed my things, hotboxed the hotel room with some of the guys, and geared up for my journey.

Being an underclassman, I received my predraft grade. Anything not in the first three rounds usually means that the athlete should head back to college for another year. Although my grade suggested I was a late-round pick, I felt ready to make the leap. I wasn't being challenged physically or mentally at the college level anymore, and with our quarterback situation uncertain, it felt like the right time to pursue my dreams.

Out of a staggering seventy thousand hopefuls, only 330 receive the coveted invitation to the NFL Scouting Combine. I was fortunate enough to be among them. To get ready, I set my sights on training with Tom Shaw in Orlando. Having worked with him before, I knew he could help me nail a top-forty time. Despite my best efforts, I was unable to convince TJeff to come with me to the Disney sports complex. And since I wanted to train together, I pivoted and decided to join him in LA.

DREAM CHASER

Sky's the limit.
—Christopher Wallace

Our prep in LA was somewhat unorganized and lackluster. And guys were distracted by the scene of the city. Our gym would periodically shut down so that a very well-known person could get their one-on-one session with no one around. We didn't have the position coaches we were promised and struggled to get time for field work. I managed to stay pretty locked in while we were there, with only one major slip-up.

One evening, we all went to dinner. Dinner led to going out, and suddenly we were at the House of Blues. Meek Mill was to perform. Around that time, Meek was one of my favorite rappers. All throughout college, we bumped *Dreamchasers 1, 2,* and *3.* We were dream-chasing so we could relate. As Meek came to the stage, a blunt was lit and passed around. The twenty-year-old me couldn't pass up the opportunity to smoke with some well-known people while watching one of my favorite artists. I hit it, passed it back, and thought nothing of it . . . until I was at the NFL Combine, and it was time to be drug-tested. Failing a drug test at a job interview is an awful look. Especially for a guy who already had a DUI on his record and was perceived as a wild boy. They notified us the night before that we'd be tested first thing in the morning. The butterflies began to kick in as I went back through my calendar, trying to figure out how many days it had been since the House of Blues. Seventeen days. I began to pray.

Although I questioned the church, I always believed in God or a higher power and relied heavily on that belief to guide and get me through. I prayed for God's will to be done and understood that it was already written. I had 6 percent body fat (THC cells stick to fat) and had been training daily, so chances were I had already sweated it out.

The NFL Scouting Combine is a week-long showcase occurring every February where college football players perform physical and mental tests in front of coaches, general managers, and scouts. They measure our height, weight, wingspan, hand length. We take an IQ test, have scheduled private meetings, and then perform on the field.

Before heading to the combine, agents help their guys get prepared. There might be odd questions teams ask. They might try to get under your skin and see how you react. Or they might get you on the whiteboard and ask about coverages and concepts. Anything was on the table. The biggest questions for me were off the field. Teams were worried about my DUI or the fact that there was a picture of me in a dress on the Internet. One team even asked if I was gay. They were trying to get a rise out of me, though this type of question was technically illegal. My key memory was being told by my agent to cut the blond out of my mohawk. I guess back then a young, Black, tattooed man expressing himself wasn't what the league was looking for.

As for the dress. In July 2012, I attended my then-girlfriend's sister's wedding. After the wedding, we went home. My girlfriend jumped in the shower and, as a joke, I popped into the dress, surprising her when she stepped out. We both got a laugh out of it. She took a picture and that was the end of it. Or so I thought. A couple days later she thought it would be funny to post the shot on Twitter. Her page was private, only a couple hundred followers. She wasn't a big football fan and didn't understand the magnitude. One of her followers was a student at Oklahoma State, one of our main rivals. They reposted it and it spread like wildfire. I was viral, posing all cute-like in a purple dress. I honestly thought nothing of it. Growing up, my older sisters would put me in wigs and dresses for fun. What's the big deal? It became a thing though. Fans of opposing teams made posters of me and brought them to games and I always had to answer questions about it from my teammates, through college and the NFL.

Let's be clear: just because someone puts on scrubs doesn't mean they're a doctor, and wearing a dress doesn't change one's gender. Clothing can be a fun and creative form of self-expression, it's simply fabric covering our bodies. The social constructs we adhere to can limit our experiences, and clothing is a prime example. I often find myself drawn to pieces in the women's section because they offer more options, better cuts, colors, and a more flattering fit. Wearing these items doesn't make me any less of a man; in fact, it helps me embrace a balance between the masculine and feminine that makes me feel whole. So, be true to yourself, wear what you want or nothing at all. All are welcome here.

I ended up being drafted in the fifth of seven rounds, with sixteen other players at my position picked before me. Were sixteen other guys better? No way. But God had a plan. I am certain OU coaches and staff told NFL scouts that I was hardheaded and liked to party. Both true, but I was also a leader and a playmaker, one of their hardest workers, and a team player. With all that said, I fell into the lap of Drew Brees and Sean Payton at the New Orleans Saints. A Hall of Fame quarterback and a Super Bowl–winning head coach. Man can't control what is already written. Hallelujah!

Being taken toward the end of the draft lit a massive fire under my ass. Conversations with my dad about how the league worked set the foundation for my mindset. I knew anyone drafted after round three had to earn their spot on the roster. At the baggage claim in New Orleans, I ran into fellow rookie and teammate Glenn Foster. He was heading to the facility as well, so I caught a ride. Glenn had a brand-new, all-white, two-door Camaro. He hopped on Airline Drive, with traffic backed up. He pulled into the far-right shoulder and put the pedal to the floor—the new whip had some gitty-up. As we were approaching a gas station, a white transporter van was making its way through the intersection. You know when it's bumper-to-bumper and oncoming traffic finally lets a car through? This was the white van, excited to finally be making his turn. He gassed it as well. Neither of the drivers saw each other. We were hit from the left side and driven into an electricity pole. The car was totaled. I wasn't wearing my seat belt but luckily the airbags deployed. I hit my left hand on the windshield, shattering the glass. Glenn's leg was pretty banged up and we were both shaken. My ears were ringing and my adrenaline was pumping. We exchanged information with the other party and made our way to the facility. We both had bumps and bruises but nothing that could keep us from competing. Because of the accident, I wore a molded cast under my glove all camp and into the season. My hands not being 100 percent added to the anxiety I already had about making the team, but hey, who said it was going to be easy?

I went to training camp every day motivated by the fear that they'd cut me. I thought if I missed an assignment or dropped a ball, that was it. This was my dream and everything I had ever worked for, and I had to earn my spot. I was rooming with former Tulane quarterback Ryan Griffin. RG and I would stay up late studying the plays and going over signals. I was lucky to have Ryan, a California kid who was already familiar with Louisiana after attending Tulane. When we had off time, he'd invite me to hang with the fam he had made locally. Introducing me to crawfish boils, inviting me to the lake, making friends outside of football. That helped with our relationship and also helped me adjust to being in a new place.

New Orleans was unlike anywhere I'd ever experienced. The air was thick and the sun felt like it was kissing my skin. So intense I half expected my tattoos to start peeling away. At practice, we'd bring out a change of clothes and cleats as we'd be drenched, with suds pouring out of our shoes around halfway through. What struck me most was the incredible fan support and the powerful bond between the team and the city, especially after the devastation of Hurricane Katrina. The way the team revitalized the spirit of New Orleans was nothing short of amazing.

That first training camp, I was one of twelve guys at my position—I had my work cut out for me. But heading into week one of the preseason, guys were going down like flies. With everyone hurt, I was to run with the first team. I ended up beginning the preseason with the ones and never looking back, starting every game of my two years with the Saints.

My adjustment to the league was not what I'd imagined. When the initial excitement of being drafted, making the team, and becoming a starter wore off, I realized how lonely the NFL could be. I was used to having an open-door policy in college, where the guys would come hang after workouts or class and play games and chill. In the NFL, most guys went home to their families. It was a job—a fun job, a high-paying job, my dream job—but I missed the comradery of college.

Luckily, Baton Rouge was right up the road. BR is where LSU is located; I made my way up there a couple times to get the SEC college experience.

I handled business like a professional from the jump. Never missing or being late to a meeting (which leads to a fine, directly deducted from your check), always knowing and executing my assignments, and handling my rookie duties. All but one. As you may or may not know, a player in their first year has to pay their dues. Those duties usually consist of small tasks throughout the year, like buying toiletries and snacks for the room during training camp, festively decorating during the holidays, and treating the group to a steak dinner. Nothing is off-limits, it just depends on the leaders of your group and how badly they were hazed by *their* OGs. I was lucky to have a laid-back group of guys in Marques Colston and Lance Moore. I was hardheaded but understood the rite of passage. To keep from being triggered, I got ahead of being told what to do by asking the guys what they needed. Out of all the responsibilities I had, picking up breakfast sandwiches on Saturday mornings from Mano's was most important. Being that this was the only nonnegotiable, I found a way to rebel. I showed up one morning empty-handed. In most cases, there would be repercussions—being taped to the goalpost, having your stuff thrown in the cold tub, or having IcyHot put in your jockstrap. But my group wasn't like that. Colston's look of disappointment was more than enough.

During my time in NOLA, I was fortunate to have Colston and Lance to look up to and follow. I knew that if I mimicked their routines, I would give myself the best opportunity for success. That meant using their massage and stretch person, reluctantly waking up earlier and getting my lift in before practice, and even staying late to get dry-needled. Ouch! Almost everything they did, I did.

I joined the team to be the speedster, the guy who would stretch the field and make those game-changing plays. But as the Saints coaching staff grew more confident in me, I started getting the same plays that Lance usually ran. To my surprise, he handled it with incredible grace. He took me under his wing, sharing tips on footwork, releases, and route adjustments, everything I needed to step up my game. Off the field, he helped me navigate the complexities of the business side of football, shaping my perspective and attitude.

Lance could have easily played the role of the gatekeeper, resenting my rise and feeling threatened by it. But instead, he understood the bigger picture: they were paying me a fraction of what he earned, and that was a clear signal of things to come. I genuinely appreciate him for being such a stand-up guy; it's rare to find that kind of support in a competitive environment. In our sport, we're all vying for a spot, yet we're also teammates. Our success is tied to each other; whoever's on the field needs to thrive for the entire team to succeed. Lance was a model teammate, and his approach to competition and collaboration laid the foundation for the professional I became.

(Love you, Sensei!)

Playing with a future first-ballot Hall of Fame quarterback made my job simple. All I had to do was get open. Drew Brees perfectly placed almost every ball he threw. We knew to turn to whichever side he placed the ball. If he threw it low or behind, it was for a reason. I actually also had the privilege of catching for Drew when I was in high school. (He had no recollection but I have picture proof.) He had a home in San Diego and during the offseason would occasionally need players to throw to. Then, and now, I admired his work ethic. He trained and played with a chip on his shoulder and obsessed over the details. We'd rep a route until it was perfect—like he could throw it with his eyes closed. We hit it off on the field, I knew my assignments, understood route running, timing, and spacing. And aimed to perfect the route tree. Outside of ball, I didn't really know him. He had a wife and kids and plenty on his plate. I'd spent my whole life around sports, in locker rooms and around big names. I'm not the type to get starstruck and have always felt like people are people. And I think that might've made him uncomfortable. I didn't go out of my way to be overly friendly. I did my job and moved along.

Many years after I was traded, it was communicated to me that the organization couldn't get a good read on me. Being a rookie, a late-round draft pick, they probably expected me to kiss a little ass. But that wasn't how I was raised, and at that point I didn't understand how to play "the game" with the powers that be. Was that their reason for trading me? Who knows? On the phone the day of the trade, they said they needed other key pieces on defense. Don't think those pieces ever panned out.

Coach Sean Payton was a lot more easygoing in my second stint with the Saints in 2021. I'd gained his respect as a man and as a player, but he had also changed. Sean had become more of a player's coach. Laughing and joking with guys, enjoying the process. He signed a shoe deal with the Jordan brand and his best player was the multifaceted Alvin Kamara. I had missed the radical-acceptance boat by a couple years. When I came into the league, we were getting fined for celebrations and suspended for smoking weed. NFL stood for "No Fun League." They weren't selling the culture the way they are now.

My first year, SP would purposely call me "Styles" instead of Stills in team meetings. It was all a part of the hazing, but I took it as disrespect. I was taught you have to give respect to get it, no matter who you are. But he came from the Bill Parcells coaching tree, hard-nosed and egotistical. Always trying to find different ways to motivate us. Every once in a while that ego would bite us in the ass. We'd play a team who was ranked high in run defense and instead of playing to our strengths, we'd try to beat them at theirs. Other times, the staff would draw up perfect game plans, where it seemed like everything they called worked.

I was lucky to fall in the draft and be shown what a championship-caliber program looked like. Being young, I didn't realize what I had until it was gone. The relationships I'd created, the support of the fans. I thoroughly appreciated my time in the city. The Saints undoubtedly have one of the best fan bases in the NFL. Some stadiums have a nightclub in them—playing prime time in the Superdome *was* the club. People dressed in their finest, dancing and singing "STAND UP AND GET CRUNK." I'll never forget it.

GLENN FOSTER

I want my friends to understand that "staying out of politics" or being "sick of politics" is privilege in action. Your privilege allows you to live a non-political existence. Your wealth, your race, your abilities or your gender allows you to live a life in which you likely will not be a target of bigotry, attacks, deportation, or genocide. You don't want to get political, you don't want to fight because your life and safety are not at stake. It is hard and exhausting to bring up issues of oppression (aka "get political"). The fighting is tiring. I get it. Self-care is essential. But if you find politics annoying and you just want everyone to be nice, please know that people are literally fighting for their lives and safety. You might not see it, but that's what privilege does.
—KRISTEN TEA

I CANNOT BRING UP GLENN FOSTER and not touch on his tragic death. Being that we were in the same rookie class, I got to spend a bunch of time with him outside of the facility. We also once spent the week together on a Saints fan cruise to Cozumel, Mexico. Outside of the locker room is where I got to know guys. Meeting their significant others and children always gave me a better idea of who they really were. Glenn was a family man and a businessman. He was well-dressed, well-mannered, and a joy to be around. Dude was a character. I can picture him now, chest pressed out, in a pair of square glasses with gold trim. He was always laughing and joking and kept a little smirk on his face.

On December 6, 2021, Glenn was found dead in rural Pickens County, Alabama, while in police custody. The autopsy report revealed signs of neck compression and strangulation. He had initially been arrested on charges of reckless driving and resisting arrest, yet the circumstances surrounding his death raised serious questions. ESPN reported the following:

Immediately after Foster was apprehended, the lawsuit says, a Pickens County sheriff's deputy wrestled him to the ground, slamming his head into the concrete. When emergency medical personnel arrived on the scene, they recommended that Foster be given medical and mental health checks, the suit alleges, but the request was ignored . . . Later that night, jail officials called for EMS personnel to perform "a vitality check" on Foster, according to the suit. When they arrived at the jail, the suit says, they asked that Foster be immediately taken to a hospital for medical care, but the recommendation was refused.

The next day, Foster's family arrived in Pickens County and posted bail. But they soon learned that Foster would not be released because he faced a new set of charges stemming from an alleged fight with another inmate in which a jailer was slightly injured. For more than 24 hours after that, the suit alleges, officers tortured Foster. The suit says that they stripped him naked, strapped him to a chair and tased him repeatedly before choking him unconscious.

The next day, when Foster was to be driven to a hospital for a court-ordered mental health evaluation, he appeared unresponsive, the suit says. As his legs hung outside the police car that was to take him to the hospital, officers allegedly forced him into the back seat by pushing him and yanking him by the neck in what the lawsuit describes as a "chokehold maneuver."

After the approximately half-hour ride to a hospital in Northport, in Tuscaloosa County, authorities found Foster slumped over, his skin discolored, and foaming from his nostrils and mouth, the suit says. Hospital personnel pronounced him dead at the scene.

Of course, all of this was filmed—but where's the video? The new Pickens County sheriff declined comment on the suit, saying, "We don't know anything about it." How convenient. It was no secret Pickens County had a troubling pattern of police brutality. In a small county of twenty thousand people, police are using deadly force 11 percent of the time. In 2019 and 2020, three Black men were killed. And another went viral for being abused with a stun gun while in handcuffs.

Glenn's wife Pamela was quoted as saying, "There

is a history here, Glenn was not the first, the second, or the third person that they've murdered and covered up and gotten away with. We're trying to stop what happened to Glenn from continuing."

I was shocked to learn of his death. Glenn wasn't someone to disrespect authority, though he was someone who knew how to stand up for himself. Even us California kids know to watch out in those small towns in the South; anything goes there. Glenn's case is just one of many that remain unresolved. He was fortunate to leave behind enough money for his family to afford a lawyer and continue fighting on his behalf. Yet here we are, more than four years later, still without any closure.

To lose a fellow teammate and friend at the hands of the police, while simultaneously protesting this very issue, only strengthened my resolve. This could happen to any of us. The biggest gang in the US gets to murder, lie, and steal, and then get away with it, all while we foot the bill with our tax dollars.

The offseason before my third year in the NFL, I was traded to the Miami Dolphins. The website *Pro Football Rumors* reported the following:

> • *Jason La Canfora of CBSSports.com (on Twitter) heard that Saints brass had soured on Stills, prompting the trade. Many teams were surprised that he was being shopped given that his contract was so inexpensive, but that might help to explain it. Meanwhile,*

the Saints are looking to load up on draft picks.

• *Adam Beasley of the* Miami Herald *(on Twitter) heard that quarterback Drew Brees was not happy with Stills or Ben Grubbs, so it's no coincidence that they've both been shipped out.*

• *According to Armando Salguero of the* Miami Herald *(on Twitter), there were questions in New Orleans about Stills' work ethic, and he apparently enjoys the nightlife quite a bit.*

Part II

LEARNING TO BE A PRO

Throw me to the wolves and I'll return leading the pack.

The New Orleans Saints have traded wide receiver Kenny Stills to the Miami Dolphins, the team announced Friday. The deal was first reported by Rand Getlin of Yahoo Sports. New Orleans will receive linebacker Dannell Ellerbe and Miami's third-round pick in the 2015 draft.
—SPORTS ILLUSTRATED, MARCH 13, 2015

THE 2015 SEASON WOULD BE THE HARDEST and most eye-opening challenge of my career. Looking back, I realize just how comfortable I had become in New Orleans. Surrounded by Super Bowl pedigree and an all-time great quarterback, the Saints' program was built on a foundation of accountability and excellence. We pushed each other, worked together in the offseason, and I had veterans holding me to a high standard. I thought this was the way every program was run.

When I got to the Dolphins, I was the new guy, needing to learn the playbook and build chemistry with my teammates, but I only made a half-hearted effort. I'm not sure what it was, whether it was the staff, a lack of motivation, or something deeper within me, but I couldn't get into it. There was a certain energy at the facility that felt off, almost stagnant. And I traced it back to the head coach, Joe Philbin. Instead of creating a winning mindset, he obsessed over petty details that had no effect on the game. We weren't allowed to wear shorts with pockets or hooded sweaters. And he'd have us stand at attention or punish us for not tying our shoes during walk-throughs. It felt less like an NFL team and more like high school detention.

Even the wide receiver group, usually filled with energy and personality, felt disconnected. The position coach, a sixty-year-old man who had played Division III football, didn't seem to understand the nuances of our game. I'm not saying you have to play in the NFL to coach in the NFL, but there's a rhythm and an intuition that's hard to teach unless you've experienced it firsthand. At times it seemed he'd rather us lose and obey his instructions than compete as intuitive ballplayers. That was frustrating and it took the fun out of the game.

I now see how my immaturity and lack of perspective held me back. I thought I could just coast through, assuming the same formula that worked in New Orleans would work here, and that was not the case.

My first mistake would be ditching the offseason program. It was voluntary, yet there's an unspoken expectation for all of us to be there. Not showing up hurt my conditioning and my chemistry with the quarterback, and that played a part in my performance throughout the year.

In New Orleans, the system ran like clockwork, with a roster full of experienced players. I knew if I did my job, everyone else would take care of theirs.

In Miami, things were different. The team was young and leadership was lacking. Instead of stepping up and leading, I fell into a passive role and let the season unfold around me. This was where I learned what being a professional really means. It's about showing up every day, no matter what, and doing your job—not just when it's easy or going your way. True character isn't built when things go well, it's defined by what you do when things *don't* go as planned.

I saw the writing on the wall early and chose to check out. Allowing frustration to take over, I let myself mentally and physically drift. The result? One of the worst seasons of my career—dropped passes, missed assignments, and a total lack of effort. At home, I blamed everything and everyone: the coaches, the offensive line, the system. In reality, I had no one to blame but myself. My failure to lead, my lack of preparation, and my inability to rise to the challenge were all on me. And that lesson hit harder than any loss I experienced that year.

Outside of the growth after reflection, my only positive memory from that season is having a couple beers with quarterback legend Dan Marino.

Late in the year after one of our ten losses, I showered quickly and jumped on the team bus. Per usual, I made my way to the very back and popped a squat. On this night, I happened to be seated behind Dan. After a couple long sighs, he turned to me with a cold one. Definitely wasn't what I expected, but it was what I needed. A couple cold beers with one of the GOATs.

Sitting there in silence, a little shift was happening inside me. Dan didn't say a word but I could feel the weight of his experience in that moment. Seventeen seasons in the NFL and he knew that sometimes things just don't go your way. Sure, things weren't going as planned, but I had so much to be thankful for. I was healthy, playing the game I loved, and learning lessons I couldn't have learned any other way. I realized then that in both sports and life, not everything is going to go my way, but the key is to keep showing up, keep grinding and giving thanks.

That offseason, I did some soul-searching. With a contract year on the horizon, I was desperate to leave the previous season behind me. But first I had to face some hard truths. I looked in the mirror and understood the only person I could control was *me*. It wasn't about blaming coaches, teammates, or anything else anymore. I couldn't control how things played out but I could control my attitude, my effort, and the way I approached each day. Going into 2016, my mission was simple: outwork everyone. Set the standard, sharpen my skills, and lead by example. The rest would follow if I showed up and gave it everything I had.

Fortunately, the 2016 season brought a wave of change with a new head coach, Adam Gase. Fresh from his success as the offensive coordinator for the Denver Broncos, where he helped Peyton Manning shatter records and secure a Super Bowl appearance (which they lost), Adam was stepping into his first head-coaching role. I knew this was a chance for a fresh start, so I made it a point to introduce myself early. I went up to his office, acknowledged my struggles from the previous year, and pledged my commitment to helping him bring his vision for this team to life.

The second contract for a late-round draft pick is often the chance to secure life-changing money. I was determined to show my value by doing whatever it took for the team. That meant mastering the offense, getting into peak physical shape, and staying healthy. That offseason, I committed to working daily with our strength staff, going above and beyond to prepare for the season. I stayed in South Florida to acclimate to the humidity and build chemistry with quarterback Ryan Tannehill. And I incorporated classical Pilates and Pyramid training used by soccer and rugby players to boost my stamina.

AWAKENING

If there was no money, and everything depended on your moral standards, the way that you behaved, and the way that you treated people, how would you be doing in life?
—TUPAC SHAKUR

WHILE MY FOCUS AND COMMITMENT to the team was higher than ever, there was also a presidential election cycle beginning. I was twenty-four and had never utilized my right to vote. For some reason, I felt inclined to get involved. One evening, as I scrolled through the channels, I noticed one of the first primary debates and decided to tune in.

Up to that point, I was pretty uninterested in government or politics. So I can't say I knew more than the basics. I don't remember one political conversation with either of my parents or any of the adults I was around growing up. (Maybe because it was taboo to talk about money, sex, religion, politics.) I was starting at square one. What party would I support? Which candidates do I like? John Kasich ended up being the person I connected with the most. He had a proven record in his state of Ohio and seemed fairly reasonable. Apparently, he didn't have enough charisma? Either way, policies and responses to current events were at the forefront for me as I was approaching making a decision. As I started to pay attention, I began to notice there were many incidents of police brutality being reported, with no repercussions or "justice."

At first, it seemed in some cases that the victim could have handled the situation differently, by being cooperative, deescalating, etc. But as time went on and more cases became public, it was very clear that no matter what was done, an officer could take a life with minimal consequences. With that information in mind, I grew fearful. I thought about if this happened to someone I knew and loved. And knew I had to use my voice as an athlete and someone with influence to say that we needed change.

At that time, athlete activism was gaining momentum. In the NFL, quarterback Colin Kaepernick and his teammate Eric Reid were sitting on the bench during the national anthem, joined by Seattle Seahawks player Michael Bennett. In the WNBA, Maya Moore, Seimone Augustus, Lindsay Whalen, and Rebekkah Brunson wore T-shirts that read, *Change Starts with Us: Justice and Accountability*. Then, on September 21, 2016, players from the Indiana Fever and Phoenix Mercury took a knee during the national anthem before their playoff game.

In soccer, US Women's National Team star Megan Rapinoe was also taking a knee, further amplifying the movement across sports.

Colin Kaepernick is known worldwide for kneeling during the national anthem, but as mentioned earlier, his protest actually began with him sitting on the bench. The shift from sitting to kneeling came after a conversation with teammate Eric Reid, as they looked for a way to express their stance against racial injustice and police brutality in a manner that would be both powerful and respectful.

Around the same time, Kaepernick also connected with Nate Boyer, a former US Army Green Beret. When they met in person and Kaepernick spoke about his decision to kneel, Boyer agreed that this would be a more respectful gesture, one that still carried the weight of protest while showing consideration for the military community.

Boyer initially considered kneeling alongside Kaepernick and Reid in a show of unity, but ultimately decided to stand beside them before a preseason game between the 49ers and the Chargers on September 1, 2016. Still, Boyer's presence underscored the mutual respect and open dialogue that helped shape one of the most iconic acts of protest in modern sports history. Boyer later admitted he couldn't have predicted the intense backlash that followed. In fact, he said he "never could've imagined the response," but "still firmly believes in the right to protest." This moment highlighted how easily the focus can shift away from the real issues, especially when the way someone protests becomes the center of attention.

Instead of engaging with the serious message Kaepernick was trying to send about racial inequality and police brutality, the conversation became all about whether kneeling was "disrespectful" to the flag or the military. And that's exactly what those in power wanted. By turning the protest into a debate about the *method* of protest rather than the reasons behind it, they effectively sidestepped the real issue.

This is a classic tactic used to maintain control: distract from the core problem and instead focus on the form of protest. The backlash wasn't about the injustice Kaepernick was trying to address, it was about the fact that his protest made people uncomfortable. But as we've seen time and time again, it's easier to be outraged over the *way* something is said than to address the deep-seated problems it's trying to highlight.

People might be interested to know my relationship and my connection to athletes like Maya, Colin, Eric, Megan, Michael, and others who were trying to bring attention to America's systemic issues. Some might assume that since we were all athletes, we were friends, communicating or even organizing together. But that wasn't the case.

Up until that point, I'd never met Colin, Eric, or Michael personally, aside from playing against them on the field. I was aware of their protests and the backlash they were receiving from the media. I saw the shift from sitting to kneeling, and I agreed with the approach; it seemed like a more respectful way to send their message. But aside from posting supportive messages on social media, I never had direct conversations with Maya, Megan, or any of the other athletes involved.

It's a challenge when everyone is balancing their

own busy schedules and lives. We're all spread thin with different priorities. Yet I can't help but think how much more powerful we could've been if we had come together, organized, shared a unified message, and leveraged our collective influence. There's real potential in athletes uniting for a cause, and I can only imagine the impact we could've had if we'd been able to make it happen.

From my earliest memories in sports, if someone got hurt, we'd get down on a knee. People kneel to pray, to propose, or to show respect in moments of gravity. To any reasonable person, it would make sense that kneeling, in this context, is one of the most respectful gestures a person can make. But as I quickly learned, reasonable people are often in short supply.

In this case, what should have been seen as a solemn act of respect, an act rooted in the same gesture we use to honor others, was twisted and misunderstood. The irony is hard to miss: a gesture meant to show reverence for lives lost, for injustice, for people in pain, became the very thing people chose to argue against. Instead of asking why a knee was taken, they asked why not something else. It wasn't about the act; it was about avoiding the real issue—the uncomfortable truth that we have a systemic problem in this country. We're so quick to attack the messenger rather than address the message.

THE NIGHT BEFORE

Romans 5:3–4

THE NIGHT BEFORE OUR SEASON OPENER against the Seattle Sea-hawks, I felt a strong conviction about getting involved in the protest. However, I knew it was important to consult my "team"—my mentors, my girlfriend, and my agent. I reached out to my trusted friend Rand Getlin to help craft the statement we planned to release. My girlfriend at the time encouraged me to follow my heart, while my agent and Rand advised that it might be wiser to wait until after I signed my new contract.

The person I was most concerned about talking to was Coach Joe. A twenty-plus-year marine and a man I consider a second father. The narrative being pushed by the media was that the protest was anti-military, anti-police, and anti-American. That taking a knee during the national anthem was disrespectful to all of those who have served and given their lives for this country.

With my understanding of the military industrial complex, this narrative now makes sense. If all these systems are intertwined, asking for accountability in one ultimately jeopardizes the others.

Out of respect for Coach, I wanted to hear his

perspective and give him a heads-up about my plans. We had a lengthy conversation where he expressed his concerns. Ultimately, he asked me not to take a knee, saying, "Remember, your grandfather wore that uniform. I wore that uniform. Your coaches have worn that uniform. People are dying in Afghanistan and Iraq. Don't disrespect them." I truly respected and appreciated his insight, but I couldn't shake this strong feeling in my gut. I told him I would pray and sleep on it before making the decision that felt right for me.

He was correct: my grandpa was a marine, my great uncle as well. Most, if not all, of my coaches growing up served or have had family in the armed forces. I understood they might be disappointed, but I also knew my truth—what I was doing and how I felt.

As a team captain, I asked to hold a players-only meeting the night before the game. With a couple of the guys beside me, I spoke to the team. I said something along the lines of: "I just want to let you guys know there's a group of us who are interested in getting involved in the demonstration during the national anthem. We'd love to do something as a team if you guys are interested, but we totally understand if—"

Before I could even finish my sentence, the room erupted. Guys screaming and shouting over each other. Some said they couldn't support the protest because of their military families, worried about what it might mean for them. Others were more concerned about how it could affect their paycheck. There were a few who just wanted to play football and stay out of the drama, keep things as normal as possible. And then, there were those who truly didn't give a fuck.

SEPTEMBER 11, 2016

As THE NATIONAL ANTHEM STARTED, we slipped down on one knee; I kept my right hand over my heart to show an added respect and bowed my head. Praying during the anthem has been my routine since high school. Asking for protection of both teams and guys playing all over the league. Praying for guidance, that we could all showcase our skills and give God all the glory. This time, I couldn't get through my prayer. Thoughts kept creeping in about the repercussions of our decision. My heart was beating faster than usual, my body trembling. On the outside, I tried to keep my cool, but internally I was shaken up. I knew how tumultuous the response would be. The disappointment from my family and friends. People who had helped raise me and get me to where I was. But I knew my intention—to bring awareness and change. I knew my heart—to lead with love, reason, and intentionality. Regardless, I was uneasy.

I was more nervous than I'd ever been for any game. It was the beginning of my contract year, against the well-known "Legion of Boom," an away game in one of the loudest stadiums in the NFL, and I had just taken part in a monumental protest. That nervousness led to an uncharacteristic wide-open drop and subsequent loss to the Seahawks. The loss ate me up. I knew that in order for the protest to have legs, I'd have to perform. Costing the team AND creating a scene was not a recipe for success. Not only that, but now I had a target on my back. With the loss and the drop, I thought to myself, *Maybe I made a mistake. Maybe I need to focus on my contract and leave the politics to the politicians.* A little bit of friction and I wanted to give up. I don't know what part of me thought this would be easy. I was embarrassed and apprehensive. Anxious about what others were thinking and saying. And worried about how this would affect my career and relationships. How my statement would be received and what to do next. Luckily, I had failed before; I knew the recipe for success was hard work.

The next day I went to the facility, answered questions from the media, and began that work. Catching over-the-shoulder throws from one of our equipment guys—John Sweeding. I hadn't dropped a ball like that since high school and didn't want to make a habit of it. Repetition has always been my friend. I caught as many balls as Sweed would throw and made a commitment to catch extra-deep and over-the-shoulder throws the rest of the season. (I also started to train my eyes with an online program called EyeGym. Worth checking out for those looking for that extra 2 percent.)

I didn't share my plans with anyone, but I was

determined to attend every community service event and become a vital part of the South Florida community. I understood that by showing up consistently, I could learn about people and build genuine connections. More importantly, I wanted to demonstrate that our commitment to service extended beyond game day. I knew it wouldn't happen overnight, but I was on a mission. A mission to earn my contract, educate myself, and help others. After all, if something matters to us, we make the time for it.

I wasn't alone that day; I stood (kneeled, but you know what I mean) in solidarity with Arian Foster, Michael Thomas, and Jelani Jenkins, brothers for life. Arian was well-informed when it came to issues of Black liberation and politics. We'd spend time in the locker room discussing the election and various political topics, and he always made compelling points. I noticed he was reading *The New Jim Crow* by Michelle Alexander, and he encouraged me to pick it up if I wanted to dive deeper into our conversations.

That book validated everything I was feeling. It provided me with the statistical data to back up my observations. I learned about the history of policing, the origins of slave patrols, and how Black communities are disproportionately policed despite committing the same amount of crimes as others. I discovered the differences in how crack cocaine and powdered cocaine were viewed based on the racial demographics of their users. I explored the implications of the "war on drugs," the three-strike rule, and stop-and-frisk policies. And perhaps most alarming was learning about privatized prisons and the Thirteenth Amendment, which tied everything together.

At the time, I didn't recognize it, but that intense urge to get involved was a calling I couldn't ignore. I didn't know much about the histories of social movements or how to create real change. I'd never been politically active—I hadn't even exercised my right to vote. My world had been all about sports—football, basketball, baseball, and track. When I wasn't on the field, I was either glued to video games like *Madden NFL, NCAA Football,* and *FIFA* or watching SportsCenter on repeat. I was focused on my own bubble, living in my own world.

But that mission, whether I was ready for it or not, was my wake-up call. My dad always reminds me, "To whom much is given, much is required." Who would have thought that a simple desire to vote would lead me to this moment? As the saying goes, *When you know better, do better.* It was time for me to get off the bench and step into a bigger role.

People ask why I did it. It's simple: I started to pay attention. And when I did, I felt the responsibility as someone in the public eye to advocate for change, to try to educate and ultimately create a better future. I thought this was pretty obvious, simple, and straightforward, though maybe I was being naive. I assumed if people saw what was going on, there would quickly be reform. Problem . . . Solution.

Feeling a mix of hopelessness and determination, I knew that doing nothing would lead to no change. I noticed how other athletes were using their platforms to advocate peacefully for justice, and I thought, *I can do this too*. I could stand in solidarity with the movement, work to educate others about what was happening, and push for real solutions. Driven by a blend of fear and hope, I felt compelled to act.

Reflecting on that decision, I'm truly grateful I answered the bell. I often pray for God to guide me toward His purpose, and this was a vital moment in that journey. While I had never been particularly interested in politics or activism, I was raised with a strong sense of community. Witnessing others courageously elevating awareness ignited a fire within me and I knew I had to get involved. It was an instinctual pull that I couldn't ignore. Though I was unfamiliar with the history of social movements and the intricacies of the systems at play, I felt deeply that change was necessary. I had to speak out and be a part of that change.

I learned about countless instances of Black and Brown individuals being killed by law enforcement, officers who are supposed to protect and serve. Time and again, I watched these tragic cases unfold without any real justice or accountability. Officers would receive paid leave, only to be reinstated in their positions or transferred to other departments. I was shocked and infuriated. It felt like the system was broken, like these lives didn't matter. The same institutions meant to uphold justice were perpetuating a cycle of harm, and with each new case, the weight of that reality grew heavier. This wasn't just an isolated problem; it was systemic. And it wasn't something I could ignore anymore.

Most cases don't ever make the news but here are several that made a particularly strong impact on me:

There was **Sandra Bland,** a twenty-eight-year-old woman who died in July 2015 while in police custody in Waller County, Texas. She was pulled over for a minor traffic violation, which escalated into a confrontation with the arresting officer. After being taken into custody, she was found dead in her jail cell three days later, with officials ruling it a suicide. There was evidence of foul play and an officer was later fired.

There was **Freddie Gray,** who was arrested in Baltimore, Maryland for possession of a knife, but forty-five minutes after he was transported in a van to the police station, he was found unconscious and not breathing, his spinal cord almost severed. He died seven days later while in a coma. The medical examiner's office ruled Gray's death a homicide, but the six officers charged were not convicted. Fishy.

There was **Alton Sterling,** who was shot and killed by two Baton Rouge, Louisiana police officers who claim Sterling reached for a loaded handgun in his pocket while they were trying to subdue him. Neither of those officers was charged in his death.

There was **Philando Castile,** who was fatally shot during a traffic stop in suburban Minneapolis, Minnesota by police officer Jeronimo Yanez, after Castile told him he had a license to carry a weapon and reached for his pocket. And while charges were brought against Yanez in this case, the officer was eventually acquitted.

There was **Eric Harris,** who was unarmed and on the ground when he was shot in the back and killed in Tulsa, Oklahoma by seventy-three-year-old re-serve deputy Robert Charles Bates, who confused his gun for a taser and said after the shooting, "Oh, I shot him! I'm sorry." Bates was found guilty of second-degree manslaughter and sentenced to four years in prison. FOUR YEARS. And he was released after serving eighteen months.

It seemed as if lethal force was only reserved for Black people.

Me and Santa (Tío Gopher), 1992.

Five-year-old
me rocking
a headdress
and two dead
front teeth.

Three generations of Stills men.
RIP Grandpa Willie.

With my best friend Joe, around when I started thinking I was cool.

Teammates Matt Fairbanks, Colin Jones, Devin Thurman, Joe, and myself. Not pictured: my leg in a cast—the only year of sports I missed in my life.

"The Boys" in 2008 before winning the California Interscholastic Federation championship for the first time in our school's history.

Khiry Fitzgerald

"Pretty boy" era in full effect. Old Myspace photo.

Tom Mills

Dad volunteered the year we won a championship. I've always appreciated that he never pushed me into ball—no pressure, no expectations. Just always encouraging me to do my best and give my all.

The "Cali Trio": Tony Jefferson, Brennan Clay, and me; I'm pretty sure this was all our first time seeing a horse, Texas, 2010.

Freshman year: Big 12 champions.

Junior year at OU. Anytime I had on that arm sleeve, watch out. Four TDs and the game-winner on a clutch fourth down.

Draft day. The twins flew in from Minnesota. I got the call on day three, just before they had to head back to the airport.

The car accident with Glenn Foster. Thank God for airbags. If you look closely, you'll see I cracked the windshield with my hand.

I chose to take a knee on Sunday to join Colin Kaepernick, Megan Rapinoe and others in bringing awareness to social injustice.

In no way was my action intended to be a sign of disrespect to anyone. I love my country. And I have the utmost respect for the servicemen and women who have—for hundreds of years—sacrificed on our behalf. It is because of them that we have the freedom to help give a voice to the voiceless.

But it's time for us to come together in solidarity. To acknowledge, as a national community, that we have to treat each other with more love and respect. That the overwhelming number of innocent people being killed right in front of our eyes is wholly unacceptable. And to demand justice for the victims of these often senseless acts, together.

I know there are honest, hardworking police officers out there who care deeply about protecting and serving their communities, and I sincerely thank them for the bravery and sacrifice. I also know that we can do better as Americans at protecting our most vulnerable citizens.

It is in that spirit that I will continue to take a knee before games in order to continue drawing attention to the important issues we face as a society.

Though I'll be on a knee, I'll continue to put my hand over my heart because I want to honor the people who make our country so special. Those who want us all to have the opportunity to enjoy our freedoms equally. Those who see the light in all of us.

Moving forward, my plan is to use organizations like RISE to continue educating myself and others on how we can collectively take the actions necessary to create positive change in our communities. As we travel this path together, I'll pay special attention to becoming a part of the solution in improving the relationship between law enforcement officers and the communities they serve.

Statement posted on Instagram, September 13, 2016.

God brought Lori Ludwig into my life at a crucial time, and she answered the call—the Anointed One. There aren't enough thank you's to express my gratitude!

Associated Press

The ball was thrown into double coverage but all I saw was it in a tunnel coming to me. Touchdown, Dolphins!

NBC News: "NFL Players Huddle with Owners Over National Anthem Protests," New York City, October 17, 2017.

Bringing smiles to the community during the holidays, all thanks to Ashley Gillis. She'd set it all up, and I covered the bill. It truly takes a village, Miami, 2018.

Week one of the 2018 season, Albert Wilson caught me off guard by taking a knee during the national anthem. We hadn't discussed it beforehand; his presence in that moment and beyond is something I'll never forget.

Colin Kaepernick and me at the Know Your Rights Camp, New Orleans, 2018.

The National Memorial For Peace and Justice, Montgomery, Alabama, 2018.

Cody Gless

Ryan Tannehill joining the Free Hearts organization, Nashville, Tennessee, 2018.

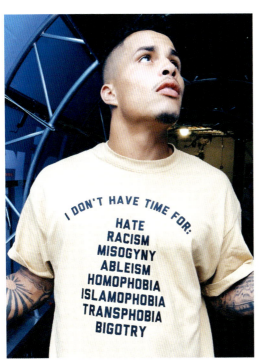

My first Pride event,
Miami, 2019.

Historically, individuals described as "brave" and "courageous" are those who face danger to protect others, explore unknown territories, or navigate uncharted waters. They often take risks that many would deem unnecessary to achieve their goals.

However, in my profession, bravery and courage is exactly what it takes to ask for help and admit you have a problem. Kenny is BRAVE. Kenny is COURAGEOUS. And since you've already made the wise decision to read about Kenny's journey, you may already know this about him. If not, you're about to find out. In the world in which I work, a world full of hurt, shame, confusion and trauma, and everything in between, Kenny's light shines like a beacon of hope guiding you through a storm. Kenny's and my paths converged at the perfect intersection of courage and curiosity, and a desire to help people for the right reasons and at the right time.

At first glance, I can imagine that many people misjudge Kenny when evaluating his physicality and presence. He is extremely bright and has been blessed with talent, wit, and athleticism, has an easy communication style and a seemingly carefree approach to life. It would be easy to assume that things that are difficult for most would come very easily to him. But I digress. You're not here for me to tell you what you already know. You're here to know the rest of the story. So, I will do my utmost to guide you through your quest to get to know Kenny, to better understand who this young man was and is, and how he became the subject of your curiosity.

My first interaction with Kenny was at an event for at-risk youth; a fact which may be surprising to some. Kenny and I began our therapeutic journey together because he approached me to ask for help—OUT LOUD and without hesitation. He asked for my card intentionally and reached out quickly to take it from my hand when I presented it to him. He was eager to begin, was always on time for his appointments, and attended because he wanted to, not because he had to. I am not certain that Kenny knew why he came to see me, initially, but he knew that he was searching for something. He wanted to know more, to understand more, to give more. It was the latter, the desire to give back, that made him extremely interesting, in my opinion.

Kenny was a young man when we began our work together. As a professional athlete, a man in his late twenties (according to some analysts) may be nearing the end of his career, but out in the real world, age is less relative. Kenny had lived many lives by the time we met, and in many ways, he was attempting to stitch them together as one would sew a patchwork quilt, in order to make one person out of the many versions of himself. In his search for truth and the desire to be kind and giving to others, he found and chose me to help guide him through this process—to help him understand the man that he was already becoming.

Like many people introduced to fame and fortune at a young age, Kenny enjoyed all the trappings that came along with it. However, Kenny did not come to see me to discuss any of these things. Even through all the parties and late nights, he carried with him the lessons he learned throughout his upbringing. Those lessons, the foundation on which he was built, continued to come to his mind—a lasting, almost nagging curiosity about the person he once was, and the man he knew he could be. He often asked me how he could be a better person and why he was stuck in certain patterns. Addressing anger and confusion were at the forefront of much of our work, as well as the desire to better understand his family, their decisions, good and bad, and the effect it had on the paths he has thus taken. Many times in our sessions we would rediscover old memories and link them to patterns in his daily routines. Kenny also had a strong attachment to his girlfriend at the time, and a fear of abandonment, while still longing for freedom without guilt—all the while asking why he would do certain things or behave in certain ways which would hurt others—while conversely having the deep desire to no longer do so.

Our sessions revolved around understanding Kenny's own needs and respecting them, while growing his confidence in himself and his ability to exist independently. Boundaries became more difficult to maintain as Kenny's fame grew and his wants and "needs" evolved in kind. Throughout all of this, Kenny's moral compass continued to point to true North, calling him to straighten his path. He continued to come into my office to ask questions and try to make sense of his desires, needs, thoughts, and to try to plan his future. With time,

Kenny's confidence in his internal self grew, and with his basic psychological needs met—safety, belonging, and self-esteem came to be. He finally began to ask the right questions toward self-actualization.

In the practice of psychology, we often say that you have to reach both ends to settle somewhere in the middle. I believe that Kenny is doing exactly this—finding his happiness and looking for his center.

Something about Kenny that captures the heart of those who are fortunate enough to get to know him is his immense capacity for gratitude and appreciation. This separates him significantly from others. Humility and gratitude are easy to forget and forego, but this comes to him naturally.

When I think of Kenny, the word namaste fills my thoughts and heart. Kenny, the light within me bows to the light within you. Namaste.

—*Dr. Ann*

This letter from psychologist Dr. Ann offers a glimpse into my journey of growth and transformation.

Volunteers for the Still Growing Summit, Miami, 2019.

Mohamed and me in the Sahara Desert.

Mohamed Quaara

COVID pull-up for Breonna Taylor, Frankfort, Kentucky,
June 2020.

Irv, Carmela, Max, and Lisa: people I know we can all count on,
Frankfort, Kentucky, June 2020.

Sitting on acting attorney general Daniel Cameron's lawn, July 2020.

Lisa Sherwood

"Good trouble"—in the words of John Lewis—with my brother Irv.

Freshly released, smoking a doobie outside the police station.

One of eighty-seven to be arrested while bringing attention to Breonna Taylor's murder, Louisville, Kentucky, July 2020.

After the NFL Players Association denied my design, I went forward with it on my own. Pregame in 2020, Kansas City, Missouri.

Black and Palestinian solidarity, Los Angeles, May 2021.

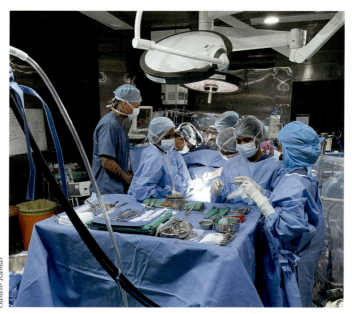

Ganesh Kumar

Viewing an open-heart surgery, Amrita Hospital, July 2023.

Ganesh Kumar

Ganesh "the selfie king" and the superheroes of the Amrita Institute of Medical Sciences, Kerala, India, July 2023.

Athletes for Ceasefire logo, designed by Jess Natale.

Omar Dreidi

National March on Washington: Free Palestine, November 2023.

Joint Statement Proposal:

In the wake of an unfolding genocide in Gaza, as described by countless legal scholars, human rights experts, and international organizations across the world, we, as athletes, recognize our moral responsibility to utilize our platform for a higher purpose—to save human lives and to raise awareness about this ongoing tragedy. We call for humanity, empathy, and an immediate ceasefire.

We are unable to turn a blind eye to the devastation being inflicted on civilians, especially children, in the Gaza Strip, through bombing campaigns funded in part by the United States. We call on President Joe Biden to call for an immediate ceasefire and to redirect those resources to address pressing domestic needs such as education, health care, and helping the unhoused.

As of February 1, and according to UN OCHA, 1,200 Israelis and 27,019 Palestinians are reported killed. Euro-Med Monitor states that among the Palestinians killed, 13,022 are children. The toll on the Palestinian population extends beyond the loss of lives, with 66,139 Palestinians reported injured, 1.9 million Palestinians displaced, and 60% of all housing units destroyed. Human Rights Watch just documented that "the Israeli government is using starvation as a method of warfare, which is a war crime.

Palestinian athletes and athletics have been acutely affected. The Palestinian Football Association says Israel has killed 88 top-tier athletes in recent months, 67 of whom played soccer, as well as 24 administrators and technical staff. Israel has also destroyed countless playing fields and gymnasiums.

Our decision to voice our concern stems from a commitment to join all those speaking up for life and dignity. We acknowledge the right of the Palestinian people to live in peace and security. As professional athletes, we underscore our shared humanity, and advocate for a path that respects all human life, regardless of religion or ethnic background.

In signing this letter, we continue a long legacy of athletes speaking up for the human rights of all people, such as Olympians John Carlos and Tommie Smith who raised their fists at the 1968 games in part to demand that apartheid South Africa and Rhodesia be held to account. We stand in the proud tradition of "The Greatest" Muhammad Ali who stood for Palestinian freedom throughout his life both in word and deed. We stand on the shoulders of these giants in our efforts to keep this tradition of athletes of conscience alive.

Our heartfelt condolences go to all families affected by this war. As athletes, we too can help build awareness and understanding and contribute to a future built on empathy and peace.

Sincerely,

(Athlete's Name)

This is the Athletes for Ceasefire statement that we sent out on February 2, 2024. We were able to gain the support of more than 250 athletes representing many different sports.

Irish and Palestinian solidarity with Irish Sport for Palestine, Dublin, Ireland, July 2024.

My immediate family on my mom's side, minus Grandma, Hendrix, and Noah, June 2021.

Tío Gilbert: activist and community leader.

My great-uncle Gilbert de la O.

Maestro Javier and me after three days of my first time sitting with ayahuasca, Costa Rica, November 2023.

The beauty of the outdoors: my first back-country hut trip, Aspen, Colorado, January 2023.

THE WORK BEGINS

Everyone has the power for greatness, not for fame but greatness, because greatness is determined by service.
—Martin Luther King Jr.

The best way to find yourself is to lose yourself in the service of others.
—Mahatma Gandhi

Taking a knee was only the beginning. At first, we were fortunate to have the support of Miami Dolphins owner Stephen Ross, which allowed us to use team resources to organize a town hall with local leaders and start working toward real solutions. Steve was one of the few NFL owners who supported our right to protest and exercise free speech. It made sense, given his commitment to social justice through his nonprofit, RISE (the Ross Initiative for Sports and Equality). RISE's mission is to educate and empower the sports community to eliminate racial discrimination, champion social justice, and improve race relations.

After the protest, I found myself without a clear plan or road map. My main focus, as it had always been, was securing a new contract, but I also knew I had to follow up kneeling with grassroots action. The first decision I made was to invest so much into the community that the negativity surrounding the protest would be overshadowed. You could disagree with the protest, but you couldn't question the actions that followed.

At that time, my understanding of what was happening in local communities was limited. I had grown up in Cali and hadn't done much in the South Florida community in year one. So, I made it a priority to get out there at least once a week, to learn, to listen, and to contribute. I was determined to make an impact, something real, something that would last beyond the headlines.

That year, and for the rest of my time with the Dolphins, you could count on me being at the team's community service events every Tuesday. School visits, gift giveaways, holiday toy drives—paid or unpaid, it didn't matter. I'd show up unannounced, not seeking media attention nor wearing my jersey. I wasn't there to make a statement; I was there to serve. And honestly, I *needed* to serve.

Playing with the kids, talking to their families, and connecting with people in the community—amid everything going on, I realized that showing up, having genuine conversations, and simply spending time with others was a powerful way to make a difference. The focus shifted from headlines or media coverage to building authentic connections. Serving in this way gave me a sense of purpose and fulfillment that nothing else could match. It reminded me that impact isn't measured by what people see on TV, it's about the difference you make in people's lives, one small act at a time.

After listening to discussions at the town hall, and in the mindset of fostering healthy community and police relations, an initiative sparked in my mind. One speaker reminisced about how in the past, police officers would make rounds through the neighborhoods with candy, introducing themselves and getting to know the residents. Putting a face to a name, building trust, and humanizing those they served.

I thought it would be great to offer a similar opportunity. So I reached out to Panini Cards to see if they would donate trading cards for officers to hand out in their communities. They loved the idea and sent several boxes my way. I then decided to attend the officers' roll call to distribute the cards, clear up the false narrative, and officially introduce the initiative.

As much as I loved silencing thousands of fans on the road, public speaking wasn't my strong suit. I was inexperienced, the topic was sensitive, and I was talking in front of a group who was told I was anti-police. But there I was, speaking from the heart. I introduced myself to the officers about to head out for their night shift, sharing where I came from, that I respected their job, and how I understood they just wanted to go home safely to their families. I told them the protest was about holding people accountable, not about being anti-police. I wasn't against the police as a whole, I was against "code blue," the abuse of power, and the systemic failures that allowed innocent civilians to be killed without consequence. I didn't get the warmest reception, nor did they ask many questions. But they let me speak my piece, and they accepted a stack of cards to potentially distribute in their communities.

During our visit through Broward County, we attended several roll calls, but one incident stands out. I encountered a group of four officers who gave off strong "Proud Boy" energy. As I made my rounds, they refused to make eye contact or shake my hand. At first, I brushed it off with a laugh and moved on, but then I thought, *If they can't even shake my hand, what are they doing to people in the field?* That thought didn't sit right with me. I couldn't ignore it, so I reported the incident to their commanding officer.

To understand why some community leaders advocate for dismantling or abolishing the police, it's helpful to look at the history of policing in America, which has long been tied to controlling Black and Brown communities and protecting the interests of white America.

In colonial America, law enforcement was originally handled by citizens and volunteers. The first system of policing, influenced by English practices, consisted of watch groups and constables—basic social services and minimal crime control. However, these early systems were often ineffective, disorganized, and too reliant on the volunteers.

But the history of policing took a darker turn in the Southern states, where, in 1704, slave patrols were formed. These patrols had three primary functions: capturing runaway slaves, quelling slave revolts through violence and terror, and maintaining order among the enslaved. This system of control set the foundation for future law enforcement practices, which would continue to target and control Black bodies.

After the Civil War and during the Reconstruction era, newly freed African Americans faced violent resistance from white communities determined to maintain their dominance. Police forces were often used to protect the interests of white citizens, keeping Black communities segregated, intimidated, and subjugated. The demand for free labor in the rebuilding of the South led to the exploitation of Black people once again, this time through the prison system. This laid the groundwork for the "Black Codes" and convict leasing, practices that kept Black people in forced labor.

Jim Crow laws further entrenched racial segregation and discrimination, with the criminal justice system playing a key role in reinforcing the social hierarchy. A loophole in the Thirteenth Amendment, which abolished slavery "except as a punishment for crime," allowed for the continued criminalization and exploitation of Black people. Policing became a tool to round up Black individuals for minor offenses under the guise of enforcing these racist laws.

When the Civil Rights Movement emerged in the 1950s and '60s, police were once again on the front lines, not as protectors of peace but as enforcers of the status quo, often violently suppressing protests and demonstrations. Police forces were tasked with maintaining order at the expense of Black lives, defending America's economic interests rather than human rights.

In the present day, the remnants of this history persist. Policies like "stop and frisk," racial profiling, and the "war on drugs" disproportionately target people of color, reinforcing the same social structures that were built on the exploitation and criminalization of Black and Brown bodies.

So when community leaders call for the abolition of the police, it's not out of some abstract or radical ideology. It's about recognizing that the institution of policing, as it currently exists, has deep roots in a system designed to protect the economic and racial status quo, often at the expense of marginalized communities. To create a truly safe and just society for all, we must reckon with this history and question whether a system built on control and oppression can ever be reformed into one that truly serves and protects *everyone*.

SOLIDARITY

We are not what we think or say we are, not what we hope,
not what we pretend we are. We are simply what we do.
—KWAME TURE

DURING THE 2016–17 OFFSEASON, I found myself in limbo, waiting for a new contract as the football calendar reset. The anticipation of what might come next grew overwhelming. To keep my mind off things, I stayed diligent with my training and traveled, hoping that the distraction might ease the weight of the unknown. I'd proven my worth to the Dolphins by having my best statistical season, playing in every game, and helping the team make the playoffs. But I'd also taken a strong stance, one that the league and general public did not approve of. I spent the offseason reading James Baldwin, Carter G. Woodson, Toni Morrison, and John Lewis. I watched documentaries like *Crime and Punishment*, *The Black Panthers: Vanguard of the Revolution*, *Free Angela and All Political Prisoners*, and *13th*. Most, if not all of these, focused on the American issues at hand; my scope was narrow. I was so focused on what was happening here, I didn't think of what could be happening around the world. And how the US could be playing a part in that too. I had just been awakened to the issues plaguing our country. Little did I know I was about to be thrust into one of the most immoral conflicts of our time.

That offseason, I, along with fourteen other NFL players, was invited on a "goodwill" trip to Israel. At first, I assumed it was a government-sponsored chance to showcase the Holy Land, a free trip to see a place I'd only heard about. I'd known of "birthright" trips (though not the more nationalist side) and thought this was something similar: an opportunity to experience the land firsthand. I knew nothing of the occupation of Palestine and saw this as a special chance to explore a country rich in history and culture. To me, life is about experiences and relationships, and I thought this journey would be one worth taking. Little did I know, it would turn out to be a full-on propaganda tour.

The week of the trip, a letter was written urging us to rethink this decision. The letter was signed by luminaries such as Angela Davis and Alice Walker, as well as athlete-activists like John Carlos and Craig Hodges; and organizations including Jewish Voice for Peace, the US Campaign for Palestinian Rights, and the Dream Defenders. It asked us NFL players to consider the political ramifications of a propaganda trip organized by the Israeli government that aimed to prevent players from seeing the experience of Palestinians living under military occupation. It read:

To the NFL Delegation to Israel:
We are writing to you as individuals and groups who work in support of human rights

and collective liberation and admire many of you who have been outspoken in movements for freedom and justice in the United States.

We have been especially inspired by you using your celebrity to shed light about and support various struggles including Black Lives Matter. The decision by Martellus Bennett to boycott the upcoming Patriots team visit to the White House following the Super Bowl win is especially brave and sends a clear message that one must take a stand against racism and oppression.

Based on the public dedication to social justice that many of you share, it came as a surprise to us to see that you will be going on a tour of Israel next week sponsored by the Israeli government as part of an effort to get you to "become ambassadors of goodwill for Israel." We would ask that you reconsider attending. These trips bringing celebrities to Israel are part of a larger "Brand Israel" campaign to help the Israeli government normalize and whitewash its ongoing denial of Palestinian rights. The Ministry of Foreign Affairs has dedicated a lot of resources to this campaign, which is designed explicitly to improve Israel's image abroad to counter worldwide outrage over its massacres and war crimes. Speaking about your trip, Israel's head of Strategic Affairs and Public Diplomacy, Minister Gilad Erdan, said, "The ministry which I lead is *spearheading an intensive fight against the delegitimization and BDS [Boycott, Divestment and Sanction] campaigns against Israel, and part of this struggle includes hosting influencers and opinion-formers of international standing in different fields, including sport."*

In other words, they are aiming to use your fame to advance their own agenda: an agenda that comes at the expense of the Palestinian people. Palestinians have chosen boycott as a tactic only after exhausting so many other approaches, and with the guidance of Black South Africans who called for BDS against the apartheid regime until it ended. As you are probably aware, the cultural boycott, including sports, was of particular significance in challenging apartheid in South Africa. What Palestinians face due to Israeli policies is familiar to Black and Brown communities in the United States and vice versa. That is why when activists in Ferguson were facing tear gas by police while organizing to demand justice for Mike Brown during the summer of 2014, Palestinian activists were tweeting them advice about how to deal with its effects, and people in Ferguson were holding up signs in solidarity with Palestinians under Israeli bombs in Gaza. That is why in 2015, more than 1,100 Black activists, artists, scholars, students, and organizations, including Angela Davis, Cornel West, and Talib Kweli, signed a

Black Solidarity Statement with Palestine, declaring their commitment to working "to ensure Palestinian liberation at the same time as we work toward our own." That is why more than sixty leading Black and Palestinian artists and activists, including Ms. Lauryn Hill, Alice Walker, and Danny Glover, were featured in a video highlighting challenges that both communities are confronting, including militarized policing and the prison industry. That is why in rallies across the United States today people are chanting: "From Palestine to Mexico, All These Walls Have Got to Go."

Palestinians have for decades been fighting policies similar to the ones people are protesting in cities across the United States. This May, Palestinians will mark sixty-nine years since they were forcibly displaced off their lands during the establishment of the state of Israel. Since then Israel has continued to expel, deny, and ban Palestinians, tearing apart families and keeping millions of refugees from returning home. Israel's brutal military occupation of the West Bank, Gaza, and East Jerusalem has now lasted fifty years and has included the building of illegal Jewish-only settlements on stolen Palestinian land, the construction of an apartheid wall to further keep Palestinians out, and the destruction of more than 25,000 Palestinian homes. Within Israel there is a purposeful policy to divide people based on *their nationality and religion, with more than fifty laws that privilege Jewish citizens over non-Jewish citizens. Palestinian athletes have been subject to violence by Israeli soldiers and not been allowed to travel to participate in competition, including the Rio Olympics. And this summer will mark three years since Israel's deadly assault on Gaza, when Israel dropped an estimated 20,000 tons of explosives, killing at least 2,200 Palestinians, including 500 children. All of these war crimes against Palestinians are funded by the United States, which sends at least $3.8 billion in military aid to Israel every year.*

Your trip to Israel comes at a time of growing cooperation between the US and Israeli governments, as evidenced by the close relationship between President Trump and Prime Minister Netanyahu, who both are eager to work together to continue implementing their right-wing, racist agendas. The dehumanizing language US politicians use against refugees fleeing to the United States and the decision to ban them is reminiscent of Israeli officials calling asylum seekers from Sudan and Eritrea "infiltrators" and detaining them in the desert. Your visit also comes at a time of growing public outcry against all oppressive policies. Palestinians are struggling today for their rights just like those who struggled in the US civil rights and South African anti-

apartheid movements, and just like Brown and Black communities are doing so across the United States now.

In 2005, Palestinian civil society issued a historic, rights-based call for people of conscience worldwide to stand with them and launch boycott, divestment, and sanctions (BDS) campaigns targeting Israel and institutions complicit in its oppressive policies until it complies with international law and guarantees Palestinian rights. Since the call there have been hundreds of BDS successes worldwide. Just like in other struggles, celebrities are taking a stand against Israel's crimes and supporting the Palestinian call for international solidarity. Musicians like Lauryn Hill, Talib Kweli, Roger Waters, Elvis Costello, and the late Gil Scott-Heron have canceled concerts or refused to play in Israel. Other cultural figures, including Naomi Klein, Judith Butler, Angela Davis, and Alice Walker, have joined the impressive ranks of those supporting BDS as a time-honored nonviolent tactic to achieve freedom, justice, and equality.

You now have an opportunity to speak out against the injustices facing Palestinians. We urge you to rethink your participation in this trip to Israel and the message it will send to your millions of fans who look up to you. The power athletes have in contributing to the fight for justice is evidenced in the leg-

acy of the late Muhammad Ali, who himself was an advocate for Palestinian rights. Angela Davis recently said at the Women's March in DC attended by tens of thousands of people: "Women's rights are human rights all over the planet and that is why we say freedom and justice for Palestine."

Please reconsider taking this trip to ensure you are standing on the right side of history.

Signed,
Organizations: US Campaign for Palestinian Rights, Palestinian Campaign for the Academic and Cultural Boycott of Israel, US Palestinian Community Network, the Dream Defenders, Jewish Voice for Peace, US Campaign for the Academic and Cultural Boycott of Israel
Individuals: Harry Belafonte, Angela Davis, Michelle Alexander, Danny Glover, Dr. John Carlos, Alice Walker, Craig Hodges, Mahmoud Abdul-Rauf, Bill Fletcher Jr., Alicia Garza, Marc Lamont Hill, Boots Riley, Umi Selah, Keeanga Yamahtta-Taylor, Jasiri X

A heavy feeling settled in my chest as I grasped the reality of the situation I'd been thrown into. Wasserman—my agency at the time, and the organizer of this trip—had now put me smack in the middle of a situation I wasn't prepared for. I was furious and overwhelmed, caught in a decision that clashed with my values. The weight of the world's problems suddenly felt crushing, especially without understanding how deeply interconnected our struggles truly are. At that moment, I couldn't help but think, *Isn't there enough to handle right at home?*

Looking back, I wish I had recognized the power of solidarity and the global support for Palestinians and others facing similar injustices. Not going on that trip felt like all I could manage at the time. In tears, I called my agency, frustrated with their guidance. I knew I had to back out.

The letter I received highlighted how our struggles are intertwined. It explained that the same tactics used by police in the US were being deployed by the Israeli occupation forces in Gaza. It emphasized that Palestinians were marginalized in their part of the world, and I needed to show solidarity rather than allow the Israeli government to use me as a pawn in their game. Even though I didn't fully grasp the situation, my trust in Dr. Angela Davis and Mr. Harry Belafonte made my new decision clear.

I still wonder how that trip came about. Was it their intention to nullify our work in the US and create confusion? Or was it an honest mistake by my agency? We've seen governments work together to discredit and derail movements before. Was this the case?

I'm so thankful this was brought to our attention. Endless gratitude to everyone who made it happen. This is proof that organizing has real power. Because of your efforts, myself, Michael Bennett, Carlos

Hyde, Cliff Avril, Justin Forsett, and Kirk Morrison all pulled out of the trip. Your work made this possible. Thank you!

As somewhat of an empath, connecting the dots between global struggles and resistance shifted my entire worldview. I felt the sting of shame—for my own ignorance, for the neglect of these truths. And the deep, shared hurt we often overlook. It wasn't just frustration or anger at being confronted with these facts; I felt a profound pain for all of us, past and present, bound by a history of struggle.

THE PLAYERS COALITION

Successful movements have radical, progressive
& moderate flanks . . . [W]e need grassroots
organizers & we need protesters. Find your
position & play it, but don't fight your
teammates bc they play a different position.
—EMAN ABDELHADI, ON X

WHEN THE 2016 PRESIDENTIAL ELECTION CONCLUDED and Donald Trump took office, a noticeable shift swept through white America. Overt racism, unchecked privilege, and entitlement surged to the surface. What had once lingered in whispers and shadows now echoed loudly in public spaces. Fueled by a newfound sense of permission, individuals felt emboldened to air their grievances, often targeting marginalized communities without fear of consequence. The masks had slipped, revealing truths about the systems that allowed such behavior to thrive. Rallies erupted, showcasing symbols like swastikas, while chants of "white power" echoed with chilling familiarity. This regression felt like a time warp, where phrases like "Blue lives matter" and "All lives matter" were wielded to undermine the urgency of Black lives. The catalyst? A campaign steeped in racist rhetoric. It was only a matter of time before the NFL found itself in the crosshairs of Trump's commentary.

When Trump was elected, I genuinely couldn't believe it. How could someone with such a deeply problematic history, marked by racism, fraud, and multiple business failures, be chosen to lead the country? His track record was a series of red flags. He'd faced legal challenges for racist housing practices, he ran a "university" that defrauded people, and his businesses were notorious for collapsing. His fame was largely due to a reality TV show, and he had a troubling history of alleged sexual assault. The controversies surrounding him were so numerous, it felt like we were living through an episode of *Saturday Night Live*. It made no sense. How did we, as a nation, arrive at this point?

Then, one day in September 2017, during a speech in Huntsville, Alabama, Trump weighed in on the athlete protests. He exclaimed, "Wouldn't you love to see one of these NFL owners, when somebody disrespects our flag, say, 'Get that son of a bitch off the field right now. Out! You're fired. You're fired!'" It was a moment ripped straight from his reality TV script.

Here was a president using a catchphrase from his show to incite a reaction, blending entertainment with politics in a way we'd never seen before. It left us all wondering: *Is this the new normal?*

In 2016, it had been a lonely stand; very few players were willing to take a knee—the majority of the league made that clear. But then Trump called us "sons of bitches," and suddenly the tide began to turn. Vice.com reported:

After President Trump's comments Friday that NFL players who kneel during the national anthem should be kicked out of the league, dozens of members of the league did it anyway in a dramatic show of unity. During Sunday's games, several players, owners, and team employees knelt, bowed their heads, linked arms, or stayed in the locker room while the national anthem played.

And wouldn't you know it? Team owners seized the moment to show their "solidarity" too. Watching Dallas Cowboys owner Jerry Jones, who once protested school integration in Little Rock, Arkansas, take a knee was nothing short of surreal. What the hell was going on?

I once again want to point out how those in power often shift the spotlight away from the real issues at hand. Instead of tackling police accountability, structural racism, and the prison industrial complex, everyone was now preoccupied with responding to Trump. It's a classic bait-and-switch—while we were busy reacting to his inflammatory comments, the deeper, more systemic problems we were trying to highlight got pushed to the background. Super frustrating how easily the narrative can be manipulated.

The energy shifted dramatically when Trump singled us out. Suddenly, everyone became a revolutionary, eager to take action. It was shocking; killing our people didn't seem to cross a line, but calling us "sons of bitches" did.

"Bitch" isn't a word that's thrown around lightly. While I wouldn't put it past Trump, I never expected to hear it said publicly from the leader of the "free world."

For the first time, we saw our power as players to unite and show the league what we could do together. It was a pretty simple revelation: if we all stood together, there couldn't be any real backlash—they're not gonna get rid of all of us.

In that moment, I thought we finally understood the stakes—we as players, as a collective force. But as the situation unfolded, the response felt more like a performative gesture, a one-off move to spite the president rather than a real commitment to confronting the deeper issues we were facing. Sure, it was empowering to see my peers stand up for themselves, but it ultimately missed the mark. The focus shifted from the systemic struggles we were up against to simply responding to one man. That realization was irritating, but even in that fleeting moment of unity, I couldn't help but be moved by the raw power of solidarity.

Throughout this journey, I've been on an emotional roller coaster, hopeful one moment, disillusioned the next. Moments like these, when unity seemed within reach, gave me hope, only to let me down later when the true work was never done. I learned to ride the wave, to keep moving forward, even when the path ahead wasn't clear. The unity we saw wasn't a solution; it was a surface-level response that missed the larger, more urgent fight. The more

I learned, the more I realized: The problem isn't a matter of isolated issues or quick fixes. It's a systemic issue, and no single policy can solve it. What's needed is a complete transformation of the systems that continue to perpetuate injustice, and that transformation will require all of us to stand up.

People would ask, "When will you stop taking a knee?" I didn't have an answer then, but I do now: We stop when this country stops demanding that we prove we're worthy of basic rights and dignity. We stop when the systems that continue to oppress us are fully transformed, and when justice is no longer a slogan, but a reality for every person regardless of race, class, or identity. We stop when the promises of equality, freedom, and justice that this nation claims to uphold are actually realized. Until then, the fight continues, because when people are still being killed for the color of their skin or discriminated against for who they love, the job is not finished.

As the league sought to address what they called the "kneeling problem," a meeting was convened with a small group of players and owners. Initially, the atmosphere was formal and structured. But then, one of the owners cut to the chase with a blunt question: "So, what do we have to do to get the kneeling to stop?" I glanced at Eric Reid, Julius Thomas, and Mike Thomas—we were the only ones in that room who had taken a knee.

To my surprise, another player chimed in. On principle, I felt it was crucial that any discussions about moving forward included Colin Kaepernick. How could we negotiate without recognizing his role in bringing attention to systemic racism and police violence? Didn't what the league do to him qualify as systemic racism? Excluding him felt like hypocrisy, especially when he was the one who had sparked this vital conversation. I couldn't understand why my colleagues didn't see this from the jump.

I never learned why Colin Kaepernick wasn't at the meeting. A league representative informed us that he hadn't been invited, which I suspect was tied to his ongoing lawsuit. Our group chat screenshots reveal that we, the players, had hoped for his presence. So it's unclear whether he ignored an invitation or simply didn't receive one. Either way, his absence clearly played into the league's agenda.

The initial Players Coalition group chat included about seventeen members—veteran players from across the league committed to making a difference in their communities. Over time, Malcolm Jenkins emerged as the coalition's leader. Given his existing rapport with the league, it was a natural fit for him to play that role.

Although Kap was initially part of the group chat, he rarely participated in the discussions. Most of the members gravitated toward Malcolm, given his established relationship with the league and his clear plan for action. As things progressed, Malcolm and his team proposed a marketing campaign, along with financial commitments to social justice initiatives and efforts to coordinate legislative action. With

Malcolm pressing to move forward, tensions arose between him and Colin, as they couldn't align on a path forward. As a result, Kap was removed from the group chat.

This was when things started to feel to me like a bit of a legacy play for Malcolm, an opportunity for him to advance his own vision, even if it meant moving forward without Colin's direct involvement. There was a sense of urgency, as if we needed to act quickly or risk missing our chance to make a real impact. With the season in full swing and everything happening over the phone, it was tough to get everyone aligned. I couldn't help but feel that an in-person meeting might have made a difference in helping us work through the tensions and figure out the best way to move ahead.

I believe that bolstering social justice and equality should have started with the NFL. How can they champion social justice issues while blackballing the man who brought these issues to light? Isn't that an injustice in itself? My frustration with Malcolm and the Players Coalition stemmed from their failure to see this. To me, that's why the league was content to have these men as their official spokespeople.

The NFL wanted the players who were kneeling to stand up. How could Malcolm, who never took a knee, negotiate on behalf of a group he wasn't part of? The players who were kneeling felt strongly that no negotiations should take place until Colin's situation was resolved. He needed to either be reinstated or included in the plans for the next steps.

We had the power to stand firm on this, but the group chat was divided. While many believed this issue was "bigger than Colin," which is true, I struggled to articulate that something about the whole situation just felt wrong.

A month after Kap was removed from the group chat, Eric Reid, Julius Thomas, Michael Thomas, Michael Bennett, and I were also removed because we had each retweeted Eric's sentiments:

> *The Players Coalition was supposed to be formed as a group that represents NFL Athletes who have been silently protesting social injustices and racism. However, Malcolm and Anquan can no longer speak on our behalf as we don't believe the coalition's beliefs are in our best interests as a whole.*

In my view, the Players Coalition was created to co-opt the "Take a Knee" movement. The league was eager to find a solution to address the criticism it faced from both sides regarding the protest.

Although I disagreed with how they went about things, since their inception, the Players Coalition has had a significant impact. Such as donating over fifty million dollars and fighting for policy change. The last update on their website was from June 2023, highlighting several key achievements:

> • *Advocated for the Massachusetts Student Opportunity Act, which secured $1.5 mil-*

lion in new funding for public schools in Massachusetts.
* *Supported Florida Amendment 4, restoring voting rights to 1.4 million citizens with past convictions.*
* *Helped pass Kentucky SB 4 (Breonna's Law), establishing a partial ban on no-knock warrants.*
* *Successfully advocated for California AB 256, which extends the Racial Justice Act to individuals with racially biased convictions prior to January 2021.*

I know that their impact goes far beyond any data and want to give them credit where it's due.

Having said that, their leadership ultimately lacked the boldness required to drive the change I was looking for or thought we needed. I felt they were too cooperative, easily swayed when there was something to gain, and too willing to make compromises. At this point, we held all the power. It's no surprise the league gravitated toward them—some people felt that the league flattered the players' egos and used them to drown out the more challenging perspectives.

I know those athletes care deeply about their communities and want to make a difference, but their willingness to sacrifice the integrity of the movement just didn't sit right with me. And wasn't something I could fully align with.

Over time, though, I've come to accept that everyone has a role to play in the fight for justice. Not everyone is going to be a radical, and that's okay. My role is to test boundaries, to challenge the status quo, to make people uncomfortable, and to push the limits of what's acceptable. That's what I'm committed to doing.

My stance is that progress requires honesty. We should have forced the NFL to confront its actions and take responsibility before we agreed to any deal. Without that accountability, all the other efforts remain compromised.

Can you imagine the domino effect this would've had on big corporations?

Simply throwing money at a problem without addressing its root causes provides no real closure and feels disingenuous. The league seemed to think that the coalition would significantly shift public perception, but the Roc Nation partnership, established a couple of years later, proved otherwise.

BOOTS ON THE GROUND

NO JUSTICE, NO PEACE . . .
And if there ain't gon' be no justice,
there ain't gon' be no peace.
—TAMIKA MALLORY

As SOMEONE NEW TO THE NONPROFIT SPACE, I had a lot to learn. During the first two years of the protest, I volunteered with the Dolphins and their partners at every event they had. Little did I know, the work they were doing was just scratching the surface.

Born in the Midwest and raised in California, I didn't fully grasp what life was like in the Deep South. Sure, I spent time in Oklahoma for college, which some consider part of the South, but my focus there was on ball. I also played in Louisiana, which is undeniably Southern, but again, football was my main concern. It became clear to me that in order to truly understand the struggles facing our communities, I had to educate myself about the history and current realities of the region. If I wanted to grasp the bigger picture of what was happening in this country, the South would be the place to start.

To deepen my understanding and take meaningful action, I partnered with the Gathering for Justice, a nonprofit organization founded by the late Harry

Belafonte and dedicated to advancing justice within the criminal legal system.

Mr. Belafonte was not only a legendary American singer and actor but also a powerful force for civil rights. He used both his platform and his resources to champion social justice and equality, standing alongside some of the most influential leaders and organizations of his time.

Through the Gathering for Justice, I was connected with grassroots organizations across the South, eager to understand local concerns and meet the people driving change in their communities. Jules Hoffenberg led the charge in organizing the trip, handling every detail with dedication and precision. Behind her, offering invaluable support and guidance, was Carmen Perez, the CEO of the Gathering.

Initially, I imagined it as a road trip where I could sit back, learn, and observe. But once we hit the road, I realized this journey would require more from me. I would be hosted and informed, but I was also expected to speak, share my story, and explain why I was on this trip. As we drove from Fort Lauderdale to Atlanta, I quickly began drafting my talking points. Again, public speaking wasn't something I looked forward to, but any nervousness I felt was overshadowed by the potential impact I could make.

The first year, two buddies, Max Himmelrich and Mike Hodges, joined me. We rented a Cruise America RV, stacked it with snacks, and hit the road, traveling through nine states in fifteen days.

We now had the chance to learn directly from the

experts. I wanted to hear people's experiences first-hand, to truly understand the challenges we faced and how I could contribute. Each day was different. I read to elementary school kids to encourage literacy, visited high schools to discuss the protest and community-police relations, and explored African American history museums. I attended college campus protests, after-school programs, toured youth detention centers, and spent time in an all-women's prison, as well as reintegration facilities. I sat in on cases with lawyers and met with members of various nonprofits to grasp their challenges.

I felt my greatest impact would be with teenagers. At twenty-five, I was close enough in age to relate and I had teenage nephews and nieces. My goal was to be as transparent as possible, as I believed this approach would earn their trust and respect in a meaningful way.

Toeing that line can be tricky. I faced this challenge during a talk with a high school football team in Lexington, Kentucky. The coach asked me to stress the importance of avoiding weed, so I told the players that they'd face drug-testing at both the college and professional levels, and that the easiest route would be to stay smoke-free.

However, in a more personal setting, when they asked me directly, I shared my own experience with cannabis. I explained how it has helped me manage pain, stress, anxiety, and inflammation, serving as a form of medicine that lightens the burdens of life.

I emphasized that while sacrifices are necessary

to achieve one's goals, there are also ways to effectively navigate the system. In college, we knew we'd be tested around bowl games, and in the NFL, testing occurred between April 20 and training camp. Outside of those windows, we were in the clear.

My main goal with the youth was to make sure they understood that each of their lives has a purpose. I wanted them to feel that, even if they believed no one cared, I did and I would do everything I could to help them.

During the offseasons of 2017 and 2019, we traveled through Georgia, North Carolina, Kentucky, Tennessee, Louisiana, Mississippi, and Alabama. Throughout this journey, I gained valuable insights into critical issues such as the prison industrial complex, wrongful convictions, reentry programs, bail reform, mandatory sentencing laws, privatized prisons, and the death penalty. I also learned about voter registration and participation, gentrification, affordable housing, and the ways in which these issues intersect with mental health.

One of the highlights of my journey was visiting the Equal Justice Initiative (EJI), founded by Bryan Stevenson. There, I discovered powerful efforts to end mass incarceration and exonerate the wrongfully convicted. The experience was incredibly moving, especially as I toured the museums and memorials. The displays illustrating how our ancestors were transported on ships, with haunting images from the Freedom Rides and the bombing of the Ebenezer Baptist Church, weighed heavily on me.

When I first entered the National Memorial for Peace and Justice in Montgomery, Alabama, I faced 805 steel rectangles. Each six-foot beam is engraved with the names and locations of victims of racial terrorism and lynching, marking the US counties where these horrors took place. The weight of the names on those beams was undeniable. But as I walked deeper into the space, something shifted. I realized the rectangles were actually suspended above me, each one rising higher as I walked beneath them. At first, they were hanging at eye level, accessible, as though inviting me to connect with the stories of the men and women whose names were etched into them. But as I progressed, they loomed over me, creating a sense of being surrounded, a symbolic echo of lynchings. Immersed in the weight of history.

What struck me wasn't just the names of victims, but the realization that some of them remained *unnamed*. Some had been so disfigured by brutal acts of racial terrorism that their identities were lost to history. This is the history that certain people are trying to erase: the history of racial terror, segregation, and Jim Crow, a legacy of violence and oppression that shaped this country and continues to impact us today.

Emotions surged through me: deep pain and deep rage. I was standing in a space that demanded to be acknowledged, a space that confronted me with the truth of our past. The hanging beams, with their quiet but powerful presence, made it impossible to look away.

Reflecting on the timeline of America's history,

from the brutal beginnings of slavery to where we are now, was exhausting. The weight of centuries of pain and suffering, rooted in the horrors of slavery and systemic injustice, can feel overwhelming. But no matter how heavy the burden, I always find my way back to inspiration and empowerment.

What's truly striking is not just the immense suffering that shaped our history, but the incredible resilience and perseverance of those who endured it. Enslaved people, their descendants, and countless others who have fought against racism, oppression, and inequality, have shown us what it means to survive, to resist, and to rise against all odds.

It is our responsibility to carry that torch forward, to hold America accountable to the values it claims to cherish: liberty, justice, and equality for all. Despite the centuries of injustice, despite the systems built to hold us down, we've still managed to rise. In doing so, we honor the strength and sacrifice of those who came before us. Their struggle is not just part of our past, it's the foundation upon which we must build a future of true freedom and equality.

I'm deeply grateful for the opportunity to visit these important sites and learn more about the history of the movement. I highly encourage everyone to take the time to visit places like the Equal Justice Initiative, the Birmingham Civil Rights Institute, the Lorraine Motel (where Dr. Martin Luther King Jr. was assassinated), the National Museum of African American History and Culture in DC, and any other museum that shares this vital history.

If there are organizations, schools, or families who want to make these visits a reality, I would be more than happy to help make that happen. Please reach out to the Kenny Stills Foundation, and let's work together to make these meaningful experiences available to more people.

During my second year on the road trip, I decided to share the states and dates on my Instagram account to see if any of my teammates or colleagues would want to join me. While many expressed interest, only one person actually followed through: my guy, quarterback Ryan Tannehill. Ryan met me in Tennessee, where we visited Free Hearts (an organization supporting children of incarcerated parents), toured an all-women's prison and a youth detention center, and spoke at an elementary school through Raising the Bar, an anti-gang mentorship program.

As the only white guy in the group, Ryan fully embraced the experience, even offering to speak to the youth we were working with. I could tell it might have pushed him out of his comfort zone, but he stepped up without hesitation and made a real effort. I had always respected him as a competitor on the field, but this experience revealed more of his character as a person. Sometimes, it's the smallest actions that create the biggest impacts, and I know those kids will always remember him.

Ironically, Ryan was traded to the Tennessee Titans just a month later.

Having a second year on the tour was essential.

I wanted people to understand that this wasn't just a one-time effort. And I also knew that there were many organizations busting their asses that needed support. By showing up, spending time, and highlighting their work, I was hoping we could provide a little inspiration to keep them pushing forward.

I also aimed to do more to educate my followers and supporters. In the first year, I kept cameras and media out, choosing not to publicize the trip. Even though my intentions were genuine, I didn't want anyone to think I was there for show. The second time around, however, I collaborated with the Miami Dolphins and Under Armour (one of my sponsors at the time) to create a miniseries about the journey. I believed the more people who knew about these important issues, the better informed we would all be, and perhaps that awareness could help shift some perspectives.

After my trade to the Houston Texans on August 31, 2019, my community involvement took a backseat. I was traded just a week before the season began, which meant I had to quickly learn the plays, build new relationships, and find a place to live. As a result, my engagement in the community dwindled. I managed to attend a few events, but my off days and evenings were now consumed by adjusting to my new environment.

The next year, the pandemic hit. Suddenly, our only options were to be at home or the team facility. But the issues of police brutality didn't stop. When news broke about Jacob Blake, a Black man who was shot and left paralyzed by police, I realized more had to be done. Drawing on my experience from the road trip, I knew I needed to connect with local organizers and help shine a light on their efforts.

Here I am sharing my thoughts in the aftermath, posted by ESPN on September 6, 2020:

The plan is to connect with local activists in every city. Help amplify the work they're doing and work toward making a list of demands for real change. The politicians and government officials aren't getting the job done in most cases. We have to work with the people who specialize in this work. I've been sending messages to players individually, but I want this to spread through the league. I have a list of organizers for each city for guys to connect with and make real change. I hope guys will reach out if they need information about where to start in their communities. If we connect with activists, not one time—it's not a one-time thing—but throughout this season and emphasize the work they're doing, we can make real changes in our cities. Then we can potentially put together a list of national demands and ask that the whole league support. I sent a message to [NFL executive vice president of football operations] Troy Vincent: "If we don't do something huge, what do you think is going to happen during the season as the police continue to kill our people?"

We have to be weary of teams wanting to set us up with their sheriff or mayor. It's a photo op and they can say we talked, but what is actually being done? From my perspective, I've sat down with a lot of different folks and we are still in the same place. We've twiddled our thumbs for way too long. This s— is not going to happen overnight. We understand that. This is not a pass-or-fail type of thing, but we've got to do something. It's bigger than T-shirts, kneeling, holding hands, and sitting out of practice, because that's not touching the owners' pockets.

It's important that we work with organizations outside of the NFL's network— organizations that make people uncomfortable. That's where real change comes. This isn't about who gets the credit. It's about all of us coming together and doing what's best for our people. I'm not trying to be the leader of the movement . . . We're all in this together, but this is where I'm coming from.

After this was released, a comrade, Kyle Umemba, reached out and we worked on a list of further demands, but those conversations never came to fruition.

PASSION, PAIN, AND DEMON SLAYIN'

In March 2017, before free agency had officially begun, I re-signed with the Miami Dolphins. I liked the team we had, the money being offered, the warm weather, and no state taxes. We made a verbal agreement over the phone. And for a short moment, I felt a sense of relief. We (my girlfriend at the time and I) celebrated, thinking about my life's culmination of work. Finally, financial freedom and generational wealth. I was proud but understood the expectations that came with it. And also recognized the uncertainty. I signed a four-year contract with two years guaranteed, and that's all I could expect.

With this goal accomplished, I needed to find a new source of motivation. I didn't want to end up like those players who got paid and lost their edge.

When I signed that deal, nothing about my physical world actually changed. Sure, there was this sudden shift in perception like I'd "made it." But it's not like all of life's problems disappeared the moment I put pen to paper. And honestly, I think that's what I was expecting. I was taught not to spend money before I had it, so life didn't really feel any different. I didn't have plans to buy a car or a house or celebrate in a big way. I knew I had to get back to work, back to chasing the dream of winning a Super Bowl and proving my worth.

That meant facing my blind spots, both as a player and as a person. And that's what eventually led me to look inward.

To really understand my emotional journey, you have to know that my world flipped upside down after I took that knee. We'd been sold the idea that racism was a thing of the past. In school, they showed us black-and-white photos of the Civil Rights Movement like it was ancient history. It was as if the country snapped its fingers and suddenly everyone was supportive of equality and Black liberation. And my experiences made me believe that. Being a "gifted athlete" shielded me from the reality of the world. Sure, I'd heard racial slurs here and there, but I never felt threatened by white folks or the system.

The response to the protest online was mind-blowing, far worse than I could have ever imagined. Tasteless messages from the parents of kids I grew up with, racial slurs from old classmates, and insults from complete strangers flooded my feeds.

I hadn't yet realized that the Internet isn't the best reflection of the people behind it. In face-to-face conversations, I had thoughtful, reasonable, and respectful interactions, where we could at least understand where the other person was coming from. But online, things were different. Bots and algorithms distorted reality, turning conversations into echo chambers where opinions were amplified, twisted, and manufactured. What seemed like genuine exchange was often shaped by forces beyond our control. The Internet, I came to see, wasn't a clear mirror of society, it was a distorted mirror, warping my perceptions and making the opposition seem far greater and more hostile than it actually was.

At first, I'd come home from work and spend time on Twitter, catching up on current events and seeing what people were saying. It was hard not to get caught up in all of it—mostly disdain, some threats, with bits of support sprinkled in.

I thought I was strong and tough, but reading all of that negativity was taking a toll on me. I was twenty-five, engulfed in the movement, trying to unpack my childhood experiences, and juggling a high-pressure job.

I'd achieved so many of my goals but I still felt like something was missing.

My partner's encouragement and my curiosity led me to seek help. I found myself thinking, *I've made the money, now how do I level up from here?*

I had thought money was the cure, and when I realized it wasn't, I set out to find what was.

On the inside, my default was irritable and pessimistic. I turned to substances to escape and took risks I probably shouldn't have—definitely living life on the edge. At the time, I had no idea these were signs of depression. I couldn't understand why I struggled to show love to my partner or be there for her the way she was for me. It bothered me that other people's happiness often annoyed me and that I needed substances to have a good time. Why wasn't I "happy"?

My girlfriend knew a lot of my story and had started to recognize certain behaviors. She suggested therapy. The unfamiliarity of it frightened me. Was I crazy? Was something wrong with me? It was embarrassing and uncomfortable to hear, but deep down, I knew it was something I had to accept. As much as I resisted, I couldn't ignore that it was time to face the truth.

I was reluctant but curious, so I half-heartedly started searching online. I also began devouring every self-help-themed book I could get my hands on: *Man's Search for Meaning* by psychiatrist Viktor Frankl, *Unspoken Legacy* by Claudia Black, *The Alchemist* by novelist Paulo Coelho, *The Untethered Soul* by Michael Alan Singer, *The Gifts of Imperfection* by Brené Brown, *Letting Go* by David R. Hawkins, *Attached* by Amir Levine and Rachel Heller, *The 5 Love Languages* by Gary Chapman, and more.

Each morning, I'd start my day with the *Quote of the Day* podcast by Sean Croxton, searching for inspiration. I was diving deep into understanding why I was the way I was, and where it all came from.

NEUROPLASTICITY

For one who has conquered the mind, the mind is the best of friends: but for one who has failed to do so, his mind will remain the greatest enemy.
—BHAGAVAD GITA

SOMEHOW, THE PEOPLE I'VE NEEDED have always shown up in my life. In 2017, Jen Gase asked me for an unexpected favor. Jen and I had gotten to know each other pretty well by then. I had a unique relationship with her husband, Dolphins head coach Adam Gase, and I had this habit of making friends with everyone in the building. I remembered how impactful my interactions with pros were when I was young and wanted to carry that torch forward. The Gases had three kids and I always made a point to check in on them and every other kid in the building. Because of that, Jen and I spoke more than most.

One day, she asked if I'd be willing to speak with a family member who was doing research around people from adverse family backgrounds. She told me it would take about thirty minutes after practice and then I'd be on my way.

The person Jen wanted me to speak with was Lori Ludwig. What was supposed to be a quick conversation turned into a couple of hours, and that's how I found my life coach. Lori wasn't a life coach at the time, she was running mindset programs in underserved schools. But she had the tools and she could sense my hunger for growth. After our conversation, she decided to take me under her wing. I left with a list of assignments: podcasts to listen to and books to read.

The biggest impact came from one simple task, a gratitude journal. I had to write down three things I was grateful for every day. No repeats. I could write them down or text them to her, but they had to be different each time.

This simple practice changed me in ways I never expected, and still has the most profound effect on my life. I encourage you to try it. Find an accountability partner and text each other three different things you're grateful for every night or every morning. Over time, you'll be amazed at how this small habit can shift your mindset and your life.

Lori also introduced me to the concept of *neuroplasticity*—the brain's ability to change and adapt. Until then, I'd often heard adults say things like, "I am the way I am and that's not going to change," which I took as reality. Discovering that I could change my thinking, responses, and perspectives changed the way I lived my life. Lori explained that I needed to invest in my brain just as I did in my body. Using football as an analogy, we discussed the time and effort I dedicated to my craft. If I could commit just ten minutes to an hour each day to my mental development, it would all add up and make a significant difference.

At first, I struggled with the idea of finding something new to be grateful for every day and genuinely meaning it. My mind just couldn't comprehend it. Until that point, my internal chatter had been overwhelmingly negative. I used negativity as fuel—if someone told me I couldn't do something, it only fed my desire to prove them wrong. But over time, I realized that constant negativity wasn't sustainable. It needed to be balanced out.

A lot of this mindset came from my upbringing. My parents had high expectations and pushed me to be perfect, but the positive affirmations were minimal and we rarely celebrated the small wins. I don't blame them for that. Their generation lived by the belief that they had to work twice as hard to get half as far, and that mentality shaped the way I approached life. I had to come to terms with something important: while my parents' approach helped me achieve success, it also ingrained a mindset that focused more on what wasn't going right than what was. On the outside, I projected positivity, but my inner critic was relentless—judging myself, criticizing others, and constantly focusing on the flaws in every situation. This negativity drained my energy and skewed my perspective.

Once I grew aware of this pattern, it became easier to notice the people around me whose default was joy and positivity. I could see how their outlook on life gave them more energy and helped them navigate challenges with a sense of ease. The contrast between their approach and my own was eye-opening. It made me realize the toll my pessimistic attitude had been taking on me, and it motivated me to make a change. I knew I needed to shift my mindset and embrace a more positive outlook, one that focused not just on success but on progress, growth, and gratitude.

Lori and I spent countless hours delving into my thoughts, challenging old patterns, and exploring new perspectives. But one moment in particular stands out.

One day she asked me, "When the ball is in the air, what do you think?"

I immediately replied, "*Don't drop it.*"

Her advice was to reframe that thinking: "Instead of that, tell yourself, *That's mine, and I'm going to go get it.* Imagine the ball is traveling through a tube and the person at the end of that tube is you."

I had never thought about it that way. In the past, I was either in the zone, making plays without a second thought, or obsessing over all the things that could go wrong. My internal dialogue was filled with negative affirmations: *Don't jump offside. Don't drop it. Don't miss this block.*

Shifting to this new mindset changed how I approached the game. It sounds simple, but once the ball was in the air, I focused solely on what I wanted to happen. That made all the difference.

The next step was applying that exercise to every area of my life: speaking positively and manifesting what I wanted instead of fixating on what I didn't.

The Miami Miracle meant something different for

me than everyone else. Of course, we beat the Patriots in miraculous fashion. Winning a divisional game, ruining their home-field advantage, and making their road to the Super Bowl a little more challenging. But personally, it was the day that mindset became a concept I believe and trust in the depths of my being. Lori and I were working on manifesting and keeping a positive attitude. I, like most, struggle to have positive self-talk when things go wrong. It is natural to get down on ourselves, hanging our heads, repeating that loop of *I suck, what an idiot.* Having those thoughts that don't belong or contribute to our success. So my assignment for that week was to keep the faith, regardless of what was happening—not only believe, but speak it into existence.

Like it was planned, the opportunity to put this exercise into practice came that Sunday. It was week fourteen of the regular season, a home game in Miami against the New England Patriots. As the game unfolded, it became clear that Coach Bill Belichick's strategy was to challenge me directly, placing me in single coverage for most of the game while everyone else had help or played zone. Fortunately, we had the perfect game plan, moving me around and leveraging my speed to get open. After three quarters, the game was tight.

With eleven minutes left in the fourth quarter, we faced a long second down. Second and sixteen, with a narrow lead of 28–27 as we pushed into the scoring zone. I got open on an underneath route, made my defender miss, and headed upfield.

I was so worried about protecting the football, I lost track of the first down marker and timidly went down one long yard short of the sticks. A huge mistake.

On the next play, we got stuffed, halting our drive and momentum, and we had to punt. The Patriots took over and methodically marched down the field, kicking a field goal that regained them the lead at 28–30 while eating up four minutes off the clock. Our next drive quickly stalled and with three minutes left, the Patriots had the ball again, now with a chance to make it a two-score game. With just twenty-one seconds remaining, they kicked another field goal, pushing the score to 28–33. We now needed a touchdown to win.

After receiving the kickoff, it was time for us to run our "last-second play." Ryan called out, "Gun near trips right Lexington Boise alert Newport!" We had been jokingly practicing this play during our Saturday walk-throughs ever since Adam became head coach, but never actually used it—until now.

The plan was for Ryan to throw to me on a deep in-cut. I'd make a move, pitch it to DeVante Parker, who would then get upfield and pitch it to Kenyon Drake. After that, it would be a free-for-all. Everything unfolded just as we had practiced. Once the ball reached KD, he got a couple of key blocks and was off. The only person he had to beat was Rob Gronkowski, a big, goofy, and relatively slow tight end. The Patriots made the mistake of thinking we were going for a Hail Mary, sending Gronk out to knock down a jump ball. But in a footrace, he couldn't keep up with KD. Dolphins win!

From the moment I timidly fell short of the first down earlier in the game to the instant KD crossed the goal line, the thought of losing never crossed my mind. I kept a level head and a clear mindset as I approached the sideline between series. *We got this; we're going to win this game,* I kept telling myself. This was new for me—usually, skepticism or negativity would creep in, along with intrusive thoughts about my performance or fears of letting the team down. But this time was different.

Looking back, I realize how crucial it was to speak positivity and intention into existence. This moment taught me that life doesn't just happen to us, we *make* things happen. When we focus on what's possible instead of what could go wrong, we open ourselves up to new opportunities. The goal isn't to ignore the challenges but to reframe them in a way that drives us forward instead of holding us back. A positive mindset allows us to see solutions where others might only see problems, and it empowers us to take action instead of being paralyzed by fear.

For those who don't believe in manifestation, I suppose that's why they call these moments "luck" or a "miracle." But I've come to understand that what we think about and speak into the world has a tangible impact on our outcomes. The more we nurture a positive outlook, the more we start to see results, whether it's in our relationships, careers, or personal goals. It's not just wishful thinking; it's creating a space for progress by believing in it and acting on it. Positive thoughts lead to positive actions, and those actions build the life we're capable of creating.

When KD finally scored, I fell to the ground in awe. I had believed it and it actually happened. My unwavering thoughts had come to fruition on the grand stage. If I was on the fence about the significance of mindset before, that moment solidified me as a believer for life.

I DON'T HAVE TIME FOR . . .

I alone cannot change the world, but I can cast a
stone across the waters to create many ripples.
—MOTHER TERESA

As I BEGAN TO CONNECT THE OPPRESSIVE STRUGGLES faced by various
groups, I realized how vital it was to speak out and
show my support. Sometimes, even a simple act like
wearing a T-shirt can make a significant impact. So I
decided to take that step and contribute to a larger
conversation of change.

One week, I wore a shirt to a home game that
boldly read, *I don't have time for: hate, racism, mi-*
sogyny, ableism, homophobia, Islamophobia, trans-
phobia, bigotry. The message was simple and direct:
none of these behaviors have a place in or around
me. Wearing that shirt not only affirmed my stance
on issues beyond police brutality but also opened the
door to new opportunities for intersectional unity.
Through these actions, I learned that every expression
of support counts. It's a reminder that we all have the
power to foster change, one message at a time.

In April 2019, I attended my first Pride event,
held in Miami Beach, unsure of what to expect. At
that point, I hadn't had any openly gay friends or
spent much time with anyone from the LGBTQ+

community. But I believed wholeheartedly that love is love and I wanted everyone to feel safe, loved, and supported.

As I approached the event, I was on high alert. The online threats I had been receiving had escalated from digital messages to handwritten notes that echoed the fear and hostility I had seen in civil rights museums. I received letters warning me to watch my back and hurling slurs like "porch monkey." This growing intimidation even pushed me to buy a gun for protection.

On my drive down to Florida, my mind raced with dark thoughts, particularly about the Pulse nightclub shooting in Orlando. Where back in 2016, forty-nine people were killed and fifty-three wounded in one of the ugliest hate crimes—as well as instances of gun violence—in our country's history. Living in America, such violence is always a possibility. Just as I was aware of the tragic stories of police violence against Black and Brown individuals, I knew that attacks on the LGBTQ+ community were a harsh reality. With that knowledge, I braced myself for what could potentially lie ahead.

When I arrived, it was nothing like I had imagined. To my surprise, I immediately spotted actress Gabrielle Union with her stepkids Zaire and Zaya.

This was before Zaya transitioned and before her father, basketball legend Dwyane Wade, publicly showed his support. I've admired their journey from a distance, recognizing the internal struggles they faced. I felt a sense of pride seeing someone like

Dwyane, whom we all looked up to for his incredible talent, embrace unconditional love for his child. That was a huge step in the right direction for the Black community.

After a quick photo, I hopped on the Dolphins float, in partnership with SAVE, an LGBTQ+ non-profit we'd worked with through our pregame community tailgates. The tailgates were one of the initiatives that emerged from our initial roundtable discussion. Before games, local youth and law enforcement would come together with people from all walks of life to share a meal and discuss important topics. Afterward, the kids received free tickets to attend the game.

Showing up for others is the ultimate source of fulfillment, especially in situations like this. I don't think anyone expected any players to attend, but there I was, proudly waving the rainbow flag from atop the float, fully embracing the moment.

What an incredible experience it was! The atmosphere was filled with joy and inclusivity. South Beach was alive with vibrant people celebrating love, equality, and the freedom to be their authentic selves. It was a beautiful reminder of what community and acceptance truly mean.

In the world of professional sports, there aren't many male athletes who speak out for the LGBTQ+ community, and even fewer who come out publicly. That reality is alarming, especially when you consider the statistics and the immense pressure so many feel to stay silent.

But just imagine a world where everyone could fully embrace their true selves without fear of judgment. Picture the relief, the freedom, and the positive impact this would have on our youth. Living in fear, hiding who you are—it's an impossible weight to carry. And it doesn't have to be that way.

To anyone who feels like an outcast, embarrassed or ashamed, I want you to hear this: be unapologetically yourself. Own every room you walk into and never let anyone dim your light. Your truth is powerful and it will lead you to the people who will accept you, support you, and love you for exactly who you are. There are whole communities and circles of people out there who will embrace your truth, celebrate it, and help you thrive. Me being one of them. <3

As far as I know, we only get one life.

Why spend it pretending to be someone you're not, when there's a world out there waiting for you to show up as your authentic self?

THERAPY

If you don't heal what hurt you, you'll
bleed on people who didn't cut you.
—AUTHOR UNKNOWN

MY SELF-REALIZATION JOURNEY started in my teens. I began reading books on philosophy and loved finding quotes or scriptures to ponder. Both of my parents were religious—my mom was Catholic and my dad Baptist. When I was growing up, we attended a non-denominational Christian church, but I can't say it was ever something I looked forward to. It wasn't a weekly ritual I embraced; it was more of a family tradition, especially when my parents were together. If they weren't, church visits were few and far between, mainly on the holidays. Every Sunday, I'd lie in bed, hoping they'd sleep in so I could skip going altogether.

I lacked the faith and imagination needed to believe, and the whole experience felt like an ultimatum: *Act a certain way or face eternal punishment.* That didn't sit right with me. Why did doing the right thing have to come with a threat? It felt manipulative, as if fear was the only thing keeping us in line. Once again, I found myself conflicted about being told what to do and it only deepened my skepticism.

It was also hard for me to separate the flaws of the

people from the practice itself. When I heard about lies, deceit, and the hypocrisy within the church, it made me question everything. And now, seeing people use religion as a justification for h*te, it's something I refuse to be associated with. If your God isn't loving, accepting, and inclusive of all people, then it's not a God I want anything to do with.

Regardless, I've always maintained a personal relationship with God. One that's grounded in gratitude and intention. I give thanks before meals, pray regularly, and trust in a higher power to guide me through life. Over time, my understanding of spirituality has evolved. While I once felt confined by traditional religious boundaries, I've come to realize that my path doesn't have to be defined by one specific practice or belief system.

I don't claim to have all the answers, nor do I need to. My spirituality is a blend of different traditions and practices that resonate with me personally—not because I'm trying to dilute any one faith, but because I believe in a universal truth that transcends labels. Whether it's honoring God, the earth, or the energy that connects us all, I'm guided by values of love, compassion, and radical acceptance. I don't need to know the gender, race, or specific identity of the "Maker" because I believe the divine exists beyond human constructs.

My spark for growth was influenced by two key factors: the relationship with my mother and my desire to be a better partner.

I'd been in the league for four years, retired my mom, paid off our debt, got her a house, a car—the whole package. I did it because I loved her, because she deserved it, but also because I thought it would make her happy. Back then, I didn't understand what I do now. That real happiness doesn't come from material things. Sure, those moments brought us bursts of joy . . . but lasting happiness? That comes from within. We can upgrade the house all we want, but without a solid foundation, the whole thing will eventually crumble.

I knew I needed to change my approach, but I was struggling, pulled in so many directions. I was carrying the weight of my past, the anger and isolation I felt because of the national anthem protest, and the guilt of being a lousy partner. I didn't understand how I could be living my dream yet still feel so melancholy. Where was the happiness I thought success would bring? Don't get me wrong, I had my moments, but once the buzz wore off, my baseline mood was low—frustrated, snappy, and negative. If things didn't revolve around me or if I wasn't drunk or high, I was easily triggered and quick to argue. I felt stuck in a cycle I couldn't break.

Laughing didn't come easy and, as I've mentioned, other people's joy straight-up annoyed me. *Everything* annoyed me—loud chewing, people dragging their feet; I'd nitpick over the smallest things. I was always right and my way was the only way. Characteristics that remind me of my parents.

After a few years of trying to give my mom everything, I realized that, in some ways, I wasn't actually helping. Retiring her took away one stress but added another: what to do with all that free time. And too much free time isn't always good for people.

I considered taking her on an ayahuasca retreat. I encouraged her to start new hobbies, volunteer, or even launch her own business. I pushed her to travel and see the world. But none of those were long-term solutions. That's when it hit me: I needed to lead by example and prioritize taking care of myself first. I realized that by investing in my own joy and letting it radiate, I could inspire others to do the same. From that point forward, I made self-care a nonnegotiable priority. If something or someone wasn't contributing to my growth or happiness, it had to go.

Over time, combining a life coach, therapy, and my recreational use of psychedelics (I will dive deeper into this in a later chapter), I was able to poke my head out from the cloud (depression) I lived under. It took me reaching a point of having everything and still feeling incomplete to grasp the concept that happiness is a journey, not a destination.

The hope that I had came from seeing how my partner lived. Growing up with both parents, money, and little to no trauma, she saw the world through a totally different lens. She was from the Midwest, went to a private high school, studied abroad during college, and had an eclectic group of friends. She was full of love and joy, never taking anything too serious and always seeing the positive in life. With her encouragement and my motivation to take the lead, I started to look for a therapist.

Empowered Youth (EY) was one of the local nonprofits that I worked closely with throughout my time in Miami. EY focused on enhancing the experiences of inner-city kids through life-management skills and job training. I met my soon-to-be psychologist, Dr. Ann, at one of their events in February 2018, a fundraiser in collaboration with a local chef. The boys would get to spend time in the kitchen helping prepare and serve dinner.

As everyone was getting settled, I did my rounds, making introductions and asking how each individual found themselves at this dinner. It just so happened that one of the people I chatted up at the dinner was Dr. Ann. I took her card and quickly made an appointment.

At first, I was hesitant. Getting help carried a stigma, especially in many Black and Brown communities. Therapy? That was for white folks. Why would we tell some white lady our business? How could she ever understand what we go through? I thought I was mentally and physically strong enough to work through things the same way I'd always done. I was raised to be tough and independent, so asking for help felt weak and unnecessary. Like a stereotypical dude, I didn't show my emotions and was still afraid to ask for guidance.

To make it easier on myself, I scheduled therapy sessions during the offseason. At first, I wasn't thinking about the long-term journey; I wanted to walk in, snap my fingers, and be "fixed." But it didn't work like that. Week after week, Dr. Ann pointed out my blind spots and pushed me to confront the hard truths. I was eager for change, though I didn't have the formula. Each session came with homework: exercises to try, books to read, new ways of thinking to explore. Dr. Ann didn't offer easy solutions, she challenged me, and in doing so, began to reshape my behavior and how I approached life.

One note she left me, I kept on my phone for years:

Watch your thoughts, they become words, watch your words, they become actions, watch your actions, they become habits, watch your habits, they become character, watch your character, it becomes your destiny.
—Lao Tzu

STILL GROWING SUMMIT

Along with a life coach and therapy, I started to dig into my personality—doing online personality tests (Enneagram, Myers-Briggs), getting a brain scan (NeuroCodex), and doing a full psychological evaluation. The evaluation found that the thing I called a permanent cloud was depression. I was surprised but relieved to hear that. I knew I wasn't happy, but to be depressed sounded dark. I guess I only associated depression with people who could never crack a smile or had thoughts of taking their lives. That diagnosis confirmed what I already knew—that I wasn't feeling or thinking like myself or the person I aspired to be.

After about two years of dedicated self-work, I started to come out from under that cloud. Little things that would've triggered me before, I could now work through. My negative inner chatter slowed and I began to find the silver lining in even the worst of situations.

My focus was on understanding the experiences of my childhood: the patterns and mindsets that grew from them and the coping mechanisms I could develop to heal. I took time to reflect on moments from my past. Navigating the ups and downs of a single-parent household, the weight of inherited family patterns, and my mom's relationship with alcohol. These experiences left lasting imprints, and while painful to revisit, they helped me understand how they shaped who I became.

Inside, I was tired of the inner turmoil and longed for change. To truly develop, I knew I had to face my upbringing head-on, to understand how these experiences had affected me and how they could be reframed to create a new path forward.

The practices I found most powerful in my journey became the core of a day camp for kids. Many successful athletes have foundations and host sports camps, but I wanted to go a step further. My mission was to provide kids with the mindset and strategies to thrive, no matter what challenges they face. Thinking the sooner we start nurturing our mental well-being, the better. That vision led to the creation of the Kenny Stills Foundation and, in just three months, the first Still Growing Summit. Hosting it at the historic Overtown Theater in Miami in July 2019, we welcomed over two hundred kids, along with parents and guardians, for a day centered on mental well-being and resilience. Drawing from Kap's Know Your Rights Camp, we reworked the curriculum to emphasize mental health.

The KYRC mission is to advance the liberation and well-being of Black and Brown communities through education, self-empowerment, mass mobilization, and the creation of new systems that elevate the next generation of change leaders. I had the privilege of attending and volunteering in a couple of these camps. Every time leaving armed with knowledge, a heart full of love, belonging, and a hope for the future. I connected with their work so much that in 2016 I donated the winnings from being nominated for the Walter Payton NFL Man of the Year Award to their organization.

Every part of the Still Growing Summit was planned with intention. The day began as participants arrived, each receiving a branded T-shirt and checking in their phones, a small step to encourage being present. After a healthy breakfast, we guided everyone into the theater. I'd flown in friends and family, both for their support and because I wanted them to hear my story. This was the first time I'd publicly share what I was going through.

I opened the summit with a few words about my own journey and the purpose behind the day: to equip young people with tools to prepare for life's challenges before they arise. My hope was that if kids in middle and high school could learn and practice these skills early on, they'd not only grow into strong, resilient adults but also contribute that strength to their communities.

We began with a focus on nutrition and goal-setting, leading into a powerful session on holistic wellness. KYRC family and holistic health coach Yareli Quintana shared her vision for everyone present, emphasizing that true health reaches beyond just what we eat. It's influenced by sunlight, physical activity, relationships, meditation, gut health, mental health, sleep, and even by how much time we spend on social media. She also introduced us to epigenetics, the study of how our environment and lifestyle choices can change gene expression without changing our DNA. This taught us that our choices can influence the outcome on our bodies, further empowering us to be active participants in our health journeys.

Yareli reminded us that we must be mindful not only of the food we consume but also of what we take in through our screens—our phones and televisions. She covered foods to look for, advising to aim for USDA organic or non–GMO certified options whenever possible. And if these aren't available, simply to do our best. The key takeaway was understanding food as more than just fuel; it's vital to feeding our cells, detoxing our bodies, boosting our energy, and building a strong immune system.

We then dove into the importance of gut health and the digestive system, often called our "second brain," learning that a remarkable 90 to 95 percent of our serotonin is produced in the gut. Yareli highlighted research showing that consumption of ultra-processed foods has been associated with a significantly higher risk of developing depression and ADHD, underscoring the need to be mindful of fast food and the marketing tactics that promote it.

In the US, the expense of organic and healthy foods can make it challenging to maintain a wellness-focused lifestyle. Recognizing this, we encouraged everyone to strive for better choices while also giving themselves grace along the journey to optimal health.

Yareli closed with a mantra:

I AM:
—Deserving.
—Ready to receive and currently receiving:
good health, unconditional love, infinite com-
passion, and purposeful growth in my life.

Our next speaker, Robbie Tubajon, vice president of engagement at the Pro Athlete Community, took us on a journey through core values and goal-setting, inviting us to reflect on what truly matters. "What is important to you?" He then guided us through an exercise where we listed ten things we valued, then narrowed it down to five, and finally to our top three.

For me, those values are freedom, respect, and integrity.

The call to action was to place these values somewhere visible and to communicate them with others. "We have to share these things for others to be able to help us get them," Rob reminded us. He emphasized that our values may evolve as we grow and that's completely normal.

Rob also asked, "How can we know where we're going if we're just letting life happen to us?" By setting clear goals, we create accountability, motivation, and direction. As we work toward them, they not only guide our actions but give us a way to measure our progress and success.

After covering nutrition and goal-setting, we separated the parents and children into their own spaces. I felt it was essential to give both groups room to speak openly. This separation allowed for discussions to unfold naturally, creating a safe environment for everyone. Having the parents and guardians present was crucial; we wanted both kids and adults to be speaking the same language and equipped with the same tools.

Our speakers rotated between three rooms, each addressing essential topics. Dr. Michael Lindsey, from the McSilver Institute for Poverty Policy and Research, focused on trauma, mental wellness, and self-care. He explained that mental challenges, much like physical illness, can impact how we feel, think, and act. He highlighted the prevalence of depression and anxiety among youth and explored the sources of stress, such as school pressures, bullying, gun violence, and family financial worries.

Dr. Lindsey then addressed trauma, describing it as "the lasting emotional response that often results from living through a distressing event." He identified common signs of trauma, including anger, irritability, panic attacks, pessimism, low self-esteem, risky behaviors, and overreacting to minor situations. Sound familiar?

Most importantly, he shared what we can do to cope with trauma: listen to music, spend time with friends, exercise, read, play with pets, and practice meditation or breathing exercises. And above all, he stressed that seeking help is a sign of strength, not weakness.

One of my favorite takeaways was the practical advice he offered for handling pressure. In tense situations, we can step outside, take a moment, or simply communicate that we need time and space. Not every action requires an immediate reaction, and sometimes that pause can prevent an unhelpful response. Dr. Lindsey's message reminded us that self-care is not only about building resilience but also about creating space to process emotions thoughtfully.

Lori's session centered on mindset, neuroplasticity, and gratitude, offering a powerful reminder: we can rewire our nervous system's responses to life's challenges. She explained that, contrary to popular belief, our brains are capable of change. With a growth mindset, we allow ourselves to say, "I'm learning," or, "I can't do that . . . YET." This mindset encourages a love for learning, embracing challenges, persevering through setbacks, welcoming feedback, and drawing inspiration from others' success. By contrast, a fixed mindset avoids challenges, gives up easily, rejects feedback, and feels threatened by others' accomplishments.

Lori then highlighted the impact of gratitude, sharing the quote, "Gratitude is the healthiest of all human emotions. The more you express gratitude for what you have, the more likely you will have even more to express gratitude for." She emphasized that happiness is a work ethic, requiring us to invest in our minds just as an athlete invests in their body.

She closed with a story, the Miami Miracle, illustrating the exercise in radical positivity we had been

162 ↗ STILL GROWING, STILL LEARNING, STILL ME

practicing that week. Lori's message was clear—by cultivating a growth mindset and gratitude, we can empower ourselves to face life with resilience and optimism.

Faheem Mujahid, a performance psychology coach and jack-of-all-trades, led a session on yoga and breathing exercises, giving the audience practical tools to support their wellness journey. But this was more than just an introduction to relaxation techniques; seeing a person of color lead this session held deeper significance. I wanted our audience to know that the wellness space is for everyone, not just reserved for wealthy white folks.

To reinforce this message, we ensured that every speaker at the summit, except for Lori, was a person of color. Representation in every space matters and it's powerful. I didn't fully grasp the impact of this until I saw *Black Panther* for the first time. Growing up, superheroes never resonated with me. I thought they were corny and didn't understand the excitement surrounding them. But seeing a Black superhero on the big screen changed that. It was as if a light turned on. I realized, *This is how white people must feel when they leave the theater—inspired, uplifted, and empowered.* Seeing someone who looked like me portrayed as the hero, saving the world, was exhilarating. For the first time, I saw a Black superhero who was strong, smart, and unapologetically African, on a global stage. It wasn't just entertainment. It was a reminder that we too can be the heroes of our own stories. I was so moved, I went to the theater three times.

The summit was about equipping our audience with tools for wellness, but it was also about helping them see themselves in every part of that journey.

We closed with a panel on mental health featuring three Black men. Dr. Milo Dodson, psychologist and fellow KYRC family, emceed as Lenard McKelvey (Charlamagne tha God) and I shared our experiences. I wanted our audience to see Black men openly discussing their well-being. Vulnerable, transparent, and unafraid to talk about mental health.

It's time to change the stigma around therapy, asking for help, and investing in our minds.

As our guests departed, we sent them off with goody bags full of resources, including a three-month subscription to the mental health app Headspace, a copy of *The Four Agreements: A Practical Guide to Personal Freedom* by Miguel Ruiz, a gratitude journal, a camp-branded hat, and a reusable water bottle. We provided Beyond Meat burgers, hot dogs, and Sambazon açaí bowls to show that eating well can be both nutritious and enjoyable.

That day felt like it was protected by the hands of God. Supported by friends, family, and teammates, we had no major hiccups and it was clear that everyone truly valued the information shared. It is one of my proudest moments and I'm endlessly grateful to all who made it possible.

Thank you to Kap and his partner Nessa for introducing me to the Know Your Rights family and encouraging his team's support. Thank you to my friends and family who volunteered and showed up wholeheartedly. And thank you to our guests for coming with open minds and believing in our vision. In the years to come, I'm excited to expand the summit and look forward to seeing all of you again.

After the 2019 summit I was traded, and soon after we faced the years of isolation due to the pandemic. As we all navigated lockdown and social distancing, I began to think about how to bring the next summit to life and reimagine what it could become. The passing of Congressman John Lewis, one of my heroes, led me to reflect deeply on my role in the movement.

I'd been on the "front lines," protesting at work and in the streets, even being arrested to bring attention to Breonna Taylor's case. I'd collaborated with law enforcement and grassroots organizers on finding solutions. But I began to feel that my calling was elsewhere. I found myself drawn even further into the emotional healing and personal development space, inspired by the idea of helping to revitalize people and raise consciousness. I truly believe that a society of conscious, healed individuals can lead to greater coexistence and empathy. Imagine the impact if healthier, more empathetic people filled positions of power—the ripple effect could transform our world.

This hope for a more conscious, connected humanity became my new vision.

GIRLS, GIRLS, GIRLS, GIRLS

You can't create chaos in the lives of others
and expect peace to come to yours.
—MORGAN RICHARD OLIVIER

IN MY JOURNEY TO BECOME A BETTER PARTNER and reach my highest
self, I had to first confront the way I had been conditioned to view women. There was a time when I
blindly accepted the misogynistic stereotypes society
pushed on me. Influenced by the culture and music of
the era, I saw women through a distorted lens, something to possess, conquer, and control. I treated them
as objects for pleasure, driven by jealousy and inse-
curity. I manipulated their feelings, dismissed them as
"too emotional," and focused almost entirely on their
appearance and how to get what I wanted.

I undervalued women's intelligence and contributions in so many ways, and I held them to a double
standard, particularly when it came to sex. Despite
genuinely respecting women and having been raised
by a strong mother, I was still influenced by the pa-
triarchy ingrained in society. Going inward began to
shift these beliefs in a major way. I had a realization
about equality and fairness that was overdue: If I
wanted a relationship grounded in honesty and mutual respect, I couldn't place expectations on a part-

ner that I wasn't willing to meet myself. If I wanted a judgment-free environment, I had to create it for both of us.

As I learned more about racism and how oppression operates on so many levels, I began to understand the weight of sexism and misogyny as well. I saw how women have been discriminated against, sexualized, oppressed, and dismissed for centuries.

It became clear that my complicity in this system didn't just harm women, it harmed *me* too. The narrow definition of manhood I had internalized left little room for vulnerability, emotional intelligence, or authentic connection. It's a cycle that so many of us are trapped in, one that breeds resentment and fear instead of intimacy and growth.

I had to confront the outdated beliefs I held about gender roles, like assuming a woman should be submissive or that her place was at home. That mentality wasn't just limiting; it was damaging. I'd always heard the saying *Knowledge is power*, but it wasn't enough to just know better—I had to *act* on it. So I checked myself, started actually listening to women, and began supporting their voices and goals.

I feel like I've taken ten steps back by putting all of this on paper, but it's the truth. I've been the liar, the player, and the manipulator—and carrying that toxic weight was exhausting. I was really good at doing and saying the right things, convincing the world that I had it all together. On the outside, I appeared confident and successful, but inside I was drowning in guilt and self-deception.

Growing up the way I did, I became numb to certain emotions, hiding behind a mask that kept people from seeing the real me. But as I started looking inward, I was forced to confront the reality of my actions. The guilt was overwhelming and I couldn't ignore it any longer. The weight of the lies, the manipulation, and the lack of authenticity had been slowly eating away at me, and it became clear that I couldn't move forward until I dealt with it.

This transformation has been crucial for my growth. Confronting my past actions has shown me how important it is to treat women with respect and dignity. It's not just changing behavior; it's recognizing the deeper impact of my actions and unlearning harmful patterns. To other men reading this, I invite you to examine the ways these patterns show up in your own lives. The conversations may be uncomfortable, but they are necessary. The growth is worth it. Strength lies in accountability, not avoidance.

And liberation? That's something we can only achieve together.

Part III

BRIAN FLORES AND STEPHEN ROSS

Don't write a check your character can't cash.

In 2019, THE DOLPHINS made another coaching change, hiring Brian Flores to lead the team. Flores came from the New England Patriots, a dynasty that had ruled the NFL for nearly two decades. The Patriots were known for their rigid approach, often described as a dictatorship. Flores wasted no time bringing that same mentality to Miami.

As a team captain for the previous three seasons, I assumed a mutual respect would be there, but that's why they say never to assume. Despite the tough approach, I appreciated Flores's coaching style. He was a student of the game, knowing and mastering every situation. He preached hard work and discipline like most coaches, but he stuck firm to it and held his best players to the highest standard.

The shift from Adam to B Flo was all about discipline. The organization wanted a "no nonsense" leader, a strong, authoritative figure, and hiring a man who had been instrumental in the Patriots' success was the way to signal that change.

Our relationship started to get rocky on the first day of full-padded practice. Flo came out fired up, just like every defensive player and coach, talking trash and bringing the energy. I loved it. By year six, training camp had become monotonous and I needed something to get me going.

While passing the wide receiver group during warm-ups, he shouted something like, "I wanna see which one of y'all can block, my wide receivers gotta be exceptional blockers!"

Knowing the Dolphins had beaten his former team once a year over the past four seasons, I saw an opening and went for it. "Pretty sure I was on the front side of that sixty-yard run Brandon Bolden had last year when we tapped that ass," I chirped back.

I know it sounds flagrant, given that he was the head coach, but once the door for trash talk opens, I'm sprinting through it. I don't care who it is. On the field, between those lines, it's different. And he didn't like that one bit. I'd struck a nerve.

"Shut up, Stills, you haven't done shit in this league," he replied. It got under his skin enough that he brought it up in our postpractice meeting. In classic Patriots style, we'd always have a team meeting after practice to watch film and review specifics from the day, unlike most teams, where offense and defense meet separately. But this time, Coach took it in a different direction. He belittled the team, saying things like, "Beating the Patriots was your Super Bowl," and, "No one in the NFL respects you."

The guys were stunned. They had no idea where this was coming from. After the meeting, a few players approached me, asking what happened and what I'd done. So, I told them.

I didn't realize it then, but this was only the beginning of our struggle.

With the new coaching staff came a fresh offensive coordinator, Chad O'Shea. He had joined from the Patriots as well, for his first shot as a coordinator. Chaddy O was bringing in this complex offense that had been perfected by Tom Brady, now to be run by our quarterback, Ryan Fitzpatrick. Fitzy had some familiarity with the system, thanks to his experience as a journeyman across nine NFL teams.

But as with most first-year coordinators, Chad faced challenges similar to those of a rookie QB. Training camp wasn't going smoothly and the offense was struggling. It was clear the team was under the helm of a defensive-minded head coach. Coach Flores saw this as an opportunity to get me to "focus on ball" and steer away from what he called "outside distractions."

One evening, after a long day of camp, I got called into his office. He started by telling me I was underperforming, not getting open, and that my off-field interests seemed to be a bigger priority than my work with the team. It was camp and my only "distractions" were tweeting and sharing current events on social media. It felt like he wanted to provoke me, whether to justify cutting me or simply to get in my head. I sat there, listened, and didn't give him anything to fuel the fire. I simply responded, "You're the head coach. If that's what you're seeing on the field and film, then you're right."

He was taken aback, saying, "That's it?" I nodded and we left it at that.

The way he approached the situation told me a lot about how he saw me, as a player and as a man. I thought I'd earned enough respect for a different kind of conversation. I had a track record on the field and had been nominated for the Walter Payton Man of the Year Award for my off-field work. But here he was, questioning my focus and commitment. It felt like he was drawing a line in the sand. It was his way or the highway. Whether he felt that way personally or was just following orders, my respect for him was gone.

Ironically, a few years later, he sued the NFL for its racially discriminatory hiring practices. That made me chuckle. I guess the cause only matters when it hits close to home.

In 2019, the NFL's partnership with Roc Nation and Shawn "Jay-Z" Carter took center stage.

The partnership began when it was announced that Roc Nation would help manage the NFL's Inspire Change initiative. The first major moves under this collaboration were a music showcase called "Songs of the Season" and an apparel line. The proceeds were set to fund programs aimed at improving economic empowerment, police/community relations, and criminal justice reform.

Right away, it seemed like the NFL was using Shawn as their solution to the protests, leveraging his influence to offset the impact of Colin's activism and reframe the NFL's image in Black communities. Shawn claimed he'd spoken with Kap beforehand,

and his comment "I think we've moved past kneeling" felt dismissive. He followed by saying, "I don't want people to stop protesting at all . . . kneeling is a form of protest . . . Now that we all know what's going on, what are we going to do? . . . Because the kneeling was not about a job, it was about injustice."

Apparently, Shawn also failed to recognize the grave injustice to Colin. The irony wasn't lost on me: the NFL, while blackballing Kap for protesting injustice, was now set to profit from the very issues he was calling out.

Naturally, when I was in front of the media, they asked for my reaction to the partnership and Shawn's comments. I made it a point to share my concerns honestly without putting down one man to defend the other. My first problem with Shawn was just that. He could have done his work without undermining the protest.

My guess was that this sentiment was built into the deal, especially since the NFL filmed and released his comments as a piece of the partnership's launch.

When the media asked, I told them what I thought—that he seemed out of touch. "I wonder how many common people he knows or has spoken to," I said, "if he's read my Facebook or Instagram comments or heard the things people say to me . . . To say we're moving *past* something, it didn't seem very informed."

This partnership raised real questions: Could it actually inspire change? Or was this just a feel-good campaign full of superficial gestures?

The next day, B Flo ran a Jay-Z playlist during practice. I think he was trying to distract me, get under my skin, and see how I'd respond under pressure. I suppose he didn't realize what I'd been going through. Having people scream racial slurs at me while I was kneeling in prayer made a little music feel petty.

So I laughed it off, chirping at him a few times, letting him know the playlist sucked. It wasn't just to spite B Flo or Shawn, I honestly didn't feel "Empire State of Mind" brought any energy to the field.

My reaction clearly irritated him. It got to the point where he made me do a drill I wasn't medically cleared for. But I went ahead, won the rep, then arrogantly stared him down as I trotted away.

The final straw in Miami would be me publicly calling Stephen Ross, the owner of the Dolphins, a hypocrite. I recall waking up early on the morning of August 7, 2019. As I lay in bed catching up on the news before work, I scrolled through my mentions on Twitter. Someone had tagged me in a story written about Ross. He was hosting a ten million–dollar fundraiser at his private estate for a second presidential term for Donald Trump. I was disappointed but not surprised. Stephen had gone back and forth on his opinions around the protest and our right to free speech. (The Dolphins at one point even tried to make standing for the anthem a rule in the player handbook, with those stepping out of line subject to a fine; someone ended up leaking this to the public, which led to that rule being removed.) I had made the mistake of assuming that people cared more about humanity than money, and I was wrong.

With Trump's first term, our country took major steps back, socially. White supremacists were now marching in the streets with tiki torches and running over people with cars at protests. We had the worst mass shooting targeting the LGBTQ+ community, and synagogues and schools continued to be terrorized, with no gun reform on the horizon. I thought we'd seen enough of his leadership or lack thereof.

But greed trumps all. Ross wanted to continue to pad his pockets. Saying, "I have known Donald Trump for forty years, and while we agree on some issues, we strongly disagree on many others, and I have never been bashful about expressing my opinions . . . I have been, and will continue to be, an outspoken champion of racial equality, inclusion, diversity, public education, and environmental sustainability, and I have and will continue to support leaders on both sides of the aisle to address these challenges."

It pains me to have to explain how he couldn't possibly be a champion of any of those topics. The man he was trying to put in office is the antithesis of everything that quote says. Being outspoken in support of a topic, then monetarily supporting someone opposed to it, is deranged. And somewhat clever, I guess. But money can't change the truth. Those are phony and meaningless words. His reasoning behind supporting Trump: he always made donations to support the Republican nominee, regardless of who it was.

That morning was like any other in the building; I went through my routine: sauna, breakfast, body-work, and lift. As I waited for meetings to begin, I scrolled Twitter again. And as the rest of the world started to wake up, my mentions continued to pile up, fans informing me of this fundraiser and awaiting my response. The more I thought about it, the more irritated I became. How could he have a nonprofit committed to improving race relations but support a man who has stoked racism and violence as one of the pillars of his campaign? The hypocrisy was blatant. So I decided to go to the website for RISE (Ross Initiative in Sports for Equality) and look up the mission statement: "We are a national nonprofit that educates and empowers the sports community to eliminate racial discrimination, champion social justice and improve race relations."

I screenshotted this and quote-tweeted, "You can't have a nonprofit with this mission statement and then open your doors to Trump," and hit send. I was fed up. Done with him playing the good guy publicly and doing everything he could behind closed doors to get us to stop taking a knee. Ever since we began the protest, individuals at every level of our team had been making efforts to persuade us to end it. We had a general manager "jokingly" offer us his kids and express to us that Ross would always look after us if we just stopped. I had guys on my team telling me I wasn't really Black, and that we were losing because of the protest. I even had phantom penalties called on me.

I was done. Done with receiving awards from the team and the league. Done with the surface-level community service work, and done with these uber-rich dudes thinking they could game the system. It was time for everyone to know the truth. I wanted Ross to understand that his words didn't match his actions. If he truly cared about race relations, he wouldn't be supporting a racist. That simple.

Eventually, they rebranded RISE by dropping the acronym and removing Ross's name from it. Despite the backlash, he went through with his fundraiser, which led to him being partially canceled for a hot moment. People boycotted his other businesses and vowed not to support his future ventures. It felt good to see him face some heat, to experience, in a small way, the pushback that I'd felt for decisions I made.

I think people like Ross rarely get challenged by those they employ, and almost never in the public eye. This was a lesson: when it comes to social issues, you're either all in or all out. I just wanted to know when they'd start using the same tactics they apply to influence elections and policies to actually help the Black community.

Three weeks later, on August 31, I was traded to the Houston Texans in a blockbuster deal that included myself and the Dolphins' best player, Laremy Tunsil. On the jet to Houston, Laremy and I each received a text from Ross. Laremy's was a nice farewell with an open door for him to return. Mine was a thanks for everything I'd done in the community.

It seemed clear that Stephen Ross was tired of my shit.

Leaving the Dolphins so abruptly was a bummer. I'd built real connections within the organization and the South Florida community and I didn't get a chance to say goodbye. But that's part of the business, and the Dolphins received a deal no team could refuse: five draft picks and two players. It was obvious the Texans were all in on winning, and winning now.

H-TOWN

MY FIRST WEEK IN HOUSTON was a whirlwind. We'd been traded just a week before the season opener, a Monday-night game against the New Orleans Saints. It would be my first time competing in New Orleans since I was traded back in 2015, and I was excited about the chance to play prime time in the Superdome. But I had a huge task ahead: learning a new playbook in just a few days. Luckily, head coach Bill O'Brien's system was pretty close to what I was just learning in Miami. Being from the Patriots coaching tree, his plays were the same; it was just the terminology that was different.

When I first met Bill, his assistant Jack Easterby greeted me. They both came across as the "nice white guy"—Bill, a Democrat; Jack, a pastor and former team chaplain. They did their best to make small talk and help me feel welcome, but eventually they got down to business. They explained that taking a knee wouldn't be a big deal for week one since it was an away game. But they wanted me to consider other options for the protest when we returned home in week two. I told them I'd think about it and went on my way.

I got a chance to play a bit in that first game, and even caught what should've been the game-winning touchdown with twenty seconds left on the clock. But then came Drew Brees and some terrible defensive situational football. The Saints marched down the field and kicked a walk-off game-winning field goal. Fresh start ruined. But it was a lesson for the team and an encouraging start for the new guy who had shown up less than a week ago.

As I settled in with my teammates, I was caught off guard when none other than Captain America himself, J.J. Watt, approached me. He made a point to introduce himself and expressed genuine interest in the work I was doing. Honestly, he was the last person I expected to show that kind of support, and his approval made the transition feel that much smoother. It was a gesture I didn't see coming and it helped with my comfort within the locker room.

I knew Texas was a red state, one that had a history of racist, sexist, homophobic, and Islamophobic tendencies. Florida wasn't much different, but for some reason I expected even more pushback. After all, this was the team with an owner, the late Bob McNair, who had once infamously said, "We can't have the inmates running the prison," when referring to the player protests and our demands for change.

Leading up to week two, there weren't any conversations about what was going to happen when the national anthem was played. It wasn't until Saturday night after our last meetings that I got a text about a private meeting between myself, Bill, and Jack. They once again expressed concern about me taking a knee at NRG Stadium. "No one has ever done that here. If you take a knee, I might get fired," said Bill. They asked me if there was anything else I could do. "Maybe a moment of silence or put something on the jumbotron?" I sat there and wondered, *How do I protect my integrity and also look out for them?* I truly thought about that. I appreciated them trading for me and this opportunity. We had a stacked team and a serious chance to make a run for the Super Bowl.

The best I could do was offer to sit out. I told them that I appreciated the opportunity and didn't want to mess up the comradery of the locker room or get anyone fired. But that I also had to be happy with the person I saw every day in the mirror in order to be able to perform. If they needed to release me, put me on injured reserve, or bench me, I would understand—but the action wasn't stopping.

They didn't know how to respond. How do you respond to someone who's standing firm on their principles? Someone with a strong moral compass?

I had come too far and been through too much. And to be frank, not much had changed with regard to policy and police relations. The protest was permanent. I'd stuck to my principles against mainstream America and the president, and I'd called out a team owner. I knew the risk I was taking and was ready to make the necessary sacrifices to continue to push forward.

I guess my play was worth Bill risking his job.

We had this conversation a couple other times before they actually heard me and conceded. Those conversations were more of the previous—Bill and Jack trying to find an alternative to the kneeling. As the season went on, I noticed that none of the local media covered the protest, not even taking pictures or asking postgame questions. The strategy wasn't new: *Silence the protests, don't give it any legs, and keep it from being documented.*

We finished the season in the playoffs. And then had the soon-to-be Super Bowl champions down 24–0 on their home turf. But the Chiefs made a run, scoring a touchdown and bringing the score to 24–7. On the ensuing drive, we had a quick three-and-out and instead of punting, we got greedy, ran a fake punt, and failed to convert. It was now the Chiefs' ball in the red zone. First momentum shift. On the next drive, our rookie corner got called for a questionable pass interference on Travis Kelce. That set the Chiefs up for the score, 24–14.

You might be wondering why a rookie was covering a future Hall of Famer in Travis Kelce. EGO. Our Pro Bowl safety, Tyshuan Gipson, had been suspended for our biggest game of the year. Gip was banged up and asked for a rest day and the coach responded with a rest *week*. Gip was having a career year and had Trav in check in our first meeting, holding him to four catches for fifty-eights yards and zero scores. Monumental mistake by the staff. Things were spiraling. We fumbled in our own territory on the next kickoff. Chiefs score, 24–21.

Our original game plan was to pound the ball in the run game and out-physical them, as we had earlier in the season (and beat them handily). With the game getting close again, we went away from that plan—another quick drive, Chiefs' ball with 2:57 left in the half. They moved the ball down the field and scored again. Going into halftime it was 24–28.

We never managed to get the momentum back. They would go on to score FIFTY-ONE points, so many that they ran out of celebratory fireworks. Benching Gip handicapped us. Making it harder for the defense than it already was. Not making any defensive adjustments and being predictable on offense ultimately cost us the season. The Chiefs are undoubtedly the new dynasty. And that was the year that started it. I believe that was our year and that we blew it. If there was any team I was on that should've won a Super Bowl, it was this one.

The next year, DeAndre Hopkins, our franchise wide receiver, would be traded and J.J. Watt would mutually part ways with the team. Bill O'Brien would be fired in week five. How quickly things can change.

I was released in week twelve of year two with the Texans. In the offseason we had signed two receivers, trying to replace Hop, who had been traded for crumbs. The rumor was that Jack Easterby got approval for the trade by telling ownership that quarterback Deshaun Watson no longer wanted to play with his superstar wide receiver.

HABIBI THINGS

I CAN'T SAY I TRULY BEGAN TO UNDERSTAND the Israeli occupation until I met Omar Dreidi. He came to the US for college in 2006. We were introduced in 2020, and during the pandemic we spent a bunch of time together, swapping stories, playing tennis, and getting to know one another.

He's Palestinian, from Ramallah. The kind of person who brings you gifts from home even when home is under siege. After visiting Palestine in 2023 for the first time in four years, he returned with kaffiyehs, jewelry, and sweets from the Old City. These weren't trinkets; they were cherished offerings, shared with pride and love.

That's who he is: joyful, kind, thoughtful, deeply principled. You wouldn't guess he grew up waiting at checkpoints just to get to school. That his every move was watched and harassment lurked at every corner. You wouldn't know, unless you asked.

And when I finally asked, he told me.

He spoke softly, like someone who'd learned to bury certain truths so that he could continue to move forward. He told me about soldiers raiding homes at night. About settlers and the protection they received.

About curfews, identity cards, permits, and a system designed to exhaust your will before it breaks your body.

Then he told me about the Nakba.

The catastrophe. In 1948, more than 750,000 Palestinians were expelled from their homes to make way for the founding of Israel. Hundreds of villages were erased from the land and from record. His grandparents' generation kept the keys to homes they were never allowed to return to. And the displacement didn't end in 1948. It became a system, etched into law, into borders.

A siege governs Gaza, and an occupation governs the West Bank. Omar has never been to Gaza because of that. It's just thirty miles away, but he has never crossed that short distance. Not for lack of longing, but because he is not permitted to.

Palestinians have been imprisoned, not only in Gaza's open-air cage but also in the restricted zones carved out of the West Bank, where the illusion of freedom hides the weight of constant surveillance. Checkpoints, walls, permits—these are the borders not just of land, but of daily life.

Omar never preached; he just shared. And through him and my own research, I began to come to my own conclusions. I came to understand the spirit, strength, and beauty of Palestinians, who continue to persevere through persecution.

I came to understand that resistance in Palestine is the fight to exist. It is woven into the fabric of everyday subsistence. It's raising children with joy under constant patrol. It's holding on to a house key no longer attached to a door. It is remembering when the world insists you forget.

So when I saw murals of George Floyd painted on walls in Gaza, I understood what they meant. They weren't just tributes, they were signals. *You are seen. We are with you.*

I began to understand Black-Palestinian solidarity not as a gesture or slogan, but as a shared experience. Our histories are different, but the same logic often governs our lives and deaths.

Through it all, I've seen Omar's hope flicker. I've felt his disorientation. The fear for the safety of his parents and loved ones. His questioning of whether anyone truly cares, or if this is just the reality we're all expected to live with. Especially over the past year, as we've watched video after video of families buried beneath rubble. Entire lineages gone in an instant.

As an American, born into privilege in one of the world's wealthiest and most powerful countries, I believe in the importance of understanding the world beyond my doorstep. I've read, traveled, immersed myself in cultures far from home, and connected with people whose lives are much different than mine.

Back in 2016, I walked away from a government-sponsored trip to Israel, even then sensing something wasn't right. But this time, I'm not just stepping back, I'm drawing a line. I'm putting my foot down. Speaking out. Taking a stand. It's the least I can do, and the very beginning of what I must.

Speaking to this topic specifically, the staggering amounts of funding sent to Israel, the relentless lobbying efforts by groups like AIPAC, and the way these forces shape the fate of our country all make me feel like Israel is in some ways more important than America.

It's been frustrating—devastating, actually—not being able to help in any real, tangible way. That helplessness has opened my eyes. It's helped me understand how people can be pushed to extremes, how what some call "radicalization" can really be a response to unbearable injustice.

I think about our brother Aaron Bushnell, who set himself on fire in protest. What does it mean to live in a world where someone has to do that just to be heard? And where do we go from there?

Palestine has undoubtedly changed me forever. There's no going back to the person I was before this. I've cut ties, on social media and in real life. I've let go of people who show even passive support for Zionism or white supremacy. If that's where you stand, stand far away from me.

But I hold on to some sliver of hope. Hope that the people in power will grow a conscience. Hope that something will shift. That this will end. And when that time comes, I'll be ready to show up. To help rebuild. To be part of something just.

Because doing nothing is unbearable. And forgetting is unforgivable.

BREONNA TAYLOR

*The most disrespected person in America
is the Black woman. The most unprotected
person in America is the Black woman.*
—MALCOLM X

IN EARLY 2020, AS THE PANDEMIC WAS UNFOLDING, the movement for Black lives was gaining momentum. I found myself considering whether to opt out of the NFL season to fully dedicate myself to the cause. Before making that decision, however, I wanted to seek guidance from elders. I had the privilege of speaking with some living legends—Dr. Angela Davis, Dr. John Carlos, and Steve Nash. They didn't give me direct answers, but their insights were invaluable. I left those discussions feeling grateful yet still uncertain about my path.

As I stayed ready for the season, training and attending meetings via Zoom, I was deeply inspired by the global solidarity I witnessed. People were masked up and marching through the streets, risking their lives. I needed to do more.

I started to notice how some situations received more public attention than others. This was frustrating, but it reminded me of an important lesson I learned during my first year with the Dolphins: instead of pointing fingers or complaining about what isn't being done, take initiative and get it done yourself.

I was very concerned about the details of the Breonna Taylor case and the fact that few people knew of it or were talking about it. For those who don't know, Breonna Taylor was shot and killed by police on March 13, 2020, in her Louisville, Kentucky apartment during a botched drug raid. The officers were executing a "no knock" search warrant when her boyfriend, Kenneth Walker, heard the commotion and thought they were being robbed. Kenneth then fired off a warning shot that struck a police officer. In response, police fired multiple rounds into the apartment, hitting Taylor six times.

With her case initially flying under the radar, I decided to help folks get to a demonstration in Louisville. I posted on social media about the march but also offered to pay for accommodations, gas—whatever was needed to assist people in getting there. In the end, we were able to help over thirty people pull up for the event. This demonstration was to take place on June 25 outside of the state capitol building in Frankfort, Kentucky.

I was proudly joined by friends Max Himmelrich, Irv Roland, Carmela Zumbado, and Lisa Sherwood. We thought at the last minute that it would be a powerful move to display the murderers' pictures on a sign for everyone to see. Since we were in Kentucky, finding a place that would print posters with the officers' faces on them proved challenging. Our solution? Identify a printer in a Black neighborhood.

There, we managed to get the job done. We printed poster boards featuring the faces of Myles Cosgrove, Brett Hankison, and John Mattingly, with the word *MURDERERS* boldly splashed in bloodred across them.

It was scorching on this summer day, with many folks passing out from heat exhaustion. The intensity of screaming and chanting behind a mask with the sun beating down on us was no joke. In retrospect, the gathering was quite calm for where we were with this case. Three months removed and two of the officers were still on the job—no consequences, no accountability, no charges. I flew in, unsure of what action would take place but prepared for the worst. There was minimal police presence and no response from anyone inside the capitol building. Clearly, what we were doing wasn't enough. Demonstrations like this are filled with a mix of emotions, ranging from rage to optimism and everything in between. In a perfect world, one of our government representatives would have been there, listening and trying to understand what their constituents needed. After all, they are supposed to be servants of the people. Instead, we were ignored, which only fueled our determination.

A beautiful full-circle moment was getting to see my family from the Lexington Leadership Foundation, one of the organizations I worked with on the road trips. Mr. Marcus and Chloe packed up the van and brought a group of the kids to come and support. Although tragedy pulled us together, it brought me joy to see familiar faces in the crowd and for our youth to be getting involved, using their voices in the fight for justice.

On July 8, it was announced that another demonstration would be happening, but this time with plans to "escalate." The date was set for July 14, 2020. Until Freedom, a nonprofit cofounded by Tamika Mallory, Mysonne Linen, Angelo Pinto, and Linda Sarsour, was spearheading the initiative. The plan was posted online—meeting and training at ten a.m. and action at noon. I once again was joined by Irv and Lisa. The training was nerve-racking and informative. This would be my first planned and organized action, but it wasn't Until Freedom's first rodeo.

During training, they couldn't tell us exactly what we were doing because of the possibility of undercover agents attending the meeting, a risk I hadn't considered. With everything shared on social media, anyone could be there. We were warned that we'd be taking action that could lead to arrest. While we didn't have to decide immediately, there would come a moment during the action when we'd need to make that choice. Some participants were designated as legal observers, while others were there as medical aides, lawyers, and members of the media. The level of preparation and attention to detail was reassuring. They also told us that once arrested, they would stay until every single person was released. After this training, we hopped on buses and headed to the protest.

The march began near Ballard High School in Louisville. We made our way peacefully through the streets, chanting, "*Say her name, Bre-on-na Tay-lor.*" Helicopters hovered overhead, tracking our movements, while a small group of counterprotesters tried to intimidate us with their vehicles. White male teenagers with a Confederate flag hanging off their muddy truck circled around us, revving their engine. But we didn't back down. We marched from the school to an undisclosed location until police in riot gear, wielding batons, cut us off. That's when we discovered we were near the second home of Daniel Cameron, the acting attorney general. A Black Republican, Cameron was considered a rising star in his party, groomed by Mitch McConnell himself. (His political ascent ended up being accelerated, in part, by his role in denying justice for Breonna Taylor.)

At this point, negotiations began. We were faced with a choice: disperse or risk arrest. It was decision time. Irv and I were determined to continue, while Lisa would stay on the outside to ensure our safe exit. When the police blocked our path, Until Freedom proposed a bold idea: sit on the attorney general's lawn in protest. Brilliant!

We all gathered and took our seats on the lawn, our voices rising in unison: "*No justice, no peace, pros-e-cute the po-lice!*" As the chants echoed around us, the atmosphere shifted, and slowly the arrests began. One by one, they lifted us into police vans, the process dragging on for hours. But throughout it all, we kept our heads held high, chanting and stomping our feet in defiance. Some of us even managed to keep our cell phones handy, capturing everything as we went. Our spirits remained unbroken. From the moment we hit the streets until they finally locked us in our cells nearly ten hours later, we continued to chant and sing, refusing to be silenced.

Transporting dozens of people to jail took a considerable amount of time. While we waited, they kept us in a holding area beneath the jail, cuffed together. We kept chanting and chatting as the officers stood by, armed with machine guns, treating us as if we were a serious threat. It's fascinating to observe those wielding perceived power, especially the police. You can easily spot the ones who may have been bullied as kids or those with "little man syndrome." And then there are the Black and Brown officers who believe they've gained acceptance from their white counterparts simply by wearing the uniform.

My perspective on the police has shifted dramatically from when I first tried to engage with law enforcement. I now believe that true progress requires abolition. We need to completely reimagine policing in our country. The foundation of policing is rooted in protecting white supremacy and property, and we can't reform that or change it through policy alone. I believe we must dismantle the current system and build something entirely new.

I would estimate that on that day in Louisville, we had around two hundred people with us. Eighty-seven would end up getting arrested: sixty-five women and twenty-two men.

I spent seventeen hours in a cramped cell with

twenty-one other men during a global pandemic—no masks, no social distancing. Among us were artists, professors, preachers, professional agitators, an NBA coach, lawyers, and individuals from all walks of life: Asians, whites, Blacks, and LGBTQ+ folks. We came together for one cause, and during those hours we shared our stories—who we were and how we ended up there. I was blown away by the journeys and commitment of everyone around me. After all my time in the NFL, feeling like I was shouting into the abyss, I had finally found my tribe, people who recognized that something was wrong and were ready to do whatever it took to change it.

We were fed cornbread and Kool-Aid and given old, crusty blankets. The room had bench seating all around, just enough space for everyone to sit or cuddle up together on the floor. We had no idea how long we'd be stuck in there. There was one toilet and a pay phone in the corner, which rapper Cordae kept on lock, trying to get updates and talking with his manager. Despite the circumstances, I thoroughly enjoyed every moment inside with my comrades. I felt relatively safe and in good company. I was perfectly fine hanging out and breaking bread with my new family. It was jail, after all, just a lot of waiting around for things to be processed.

The women were placed in two cells, one directly across from us and the other right next door. We managed to communicate by writing on our windows or talking through the ceiling vents. As time went on, we found out we were being held longer than expected after being charged with a felony: "intimidating a participant in a legal process." While this extended our time inside, it also helped shine a spotlight on our case. With celebrity backing, this felony charge made national news. I suspect Daniel Cameron or one of his allies wanted to teach us a lesson, which is why they threw such a hefty charge at us. It's important to note that no one was actually at his home during the protest and that it was his second residence. So who exactly were we intimidating? Their attempt to flex power ended up backfiring on them.

From the inside, "Free da guyz" and "Free da gurlz" emerged, our own phrases born out of boredom and the anticipation of our release. The next day, around nine thirty a.m., I was finally let go. I found a spot on a ledge outside the police station, went live on Instagram, and smoked a joint while I waited for the rest of the crew to be freed.

There was a team of folks waiting for us as we got out. People giving hugs and praise, folks with food and drinks. A little family reunion. Now it was time to wait and see. What would the response be?

CBS News reported:

The Louisville Metro Council opted Tuesday night to launch an investigation into Mayor Greg Fischer, his administration, and the city's police department, WLKY reports. All eleven members of the Government Oversight Committee voted to approve a probe of several issues related to Taylor's death, the Louisville

Police Department's handling of ongoing protests, and other matters.

Brett Hankison, one of the officers involved in Taylor's death, was fired on June 23, more than three months after the young woman was killed. Two other officers were placed on administrative leave. But no one was ever convicted for the killing of Breonna Taylor.

If death isn't heartbreaking enough, one of the saddest moments from my trips to Kentucky was hearing about the family support groups. I met the aunt of McHale Rose, another victim of police violence. She shared how families come together to support one another through the grieving process. Hearing her story reminded me again how police violence occurs on a daily basis, and that many cases go unnoticed by the media; some don't even get a formal investigation. Rose's aunt drove all the way from Indianapolis to be with us, demonstrating incredible resilience. I can only imagine how supporting others helps them cope, but it also makes me wonder how they find the strength to carry on amid such overwhelming grief.

On that day in July, we were joined by the mothers of Breonna Taylor and Ahmaud Arbery. Ahmaud was a twenty-five-year-old Black man who was fatally shot while jogging in Glynn County, Georgia. He was pursued by three white men who claimed they suspected him of burglarizing a nearby home. During the confrontation, they killed him with a shotgun.

So many families have lost loved ones at the hands of racism and the police. There has been no justice for Breonna, but what does justice even mean when a life is taken? No amount of money or prison time can bring someone back. Justice, then, becomes about changing the system—or, for some, taking a life for a life.

It wasn't enough for me that twenty-two of the eighty-seven people arrested were men. And it made me reflect on the role men play in social movements. Historically, we've often been given more credit than we deserve, while women's contributions have been overlooked or minimized. Women have always been at the forefront of social and political change, yet their stories are too often sidelined. I can only imagine the stories we haven't been told, stories of women's leadership, sacrifice, and resilience that have shaped history in ways we may never fully understand.

Through my journey in activism, I've come to truly understand the immense value women bring to movements. Their courage, intelligence, perseverance, and strength are the driving forces behind so much of the progress we've made. Let's not forget that it was Harriet Tubman who led the Underground Railroad, Coretta Scott King who pushed Dr. King to broaden the Civil Rights Movement into a fight for human rights. Women like Dorothy Height, Ella Baker, and Fannie Lou Hamer were the unsung heroines who built the foundation for grassroots organizing. And women played key roles in the Montgomery bus boycott, which was integral to shaping the course of history.

I am deeply grateful for their leadership and tireless efforts. As we move forward in this fight, I'm committed to amplifying women's voices and working side by side to create a more just and equitable future for everyone.

I expect all of my brothers to do the same.

Part IV

ATTACKING MY FEARS

*I learned that courage is not the absence of fear, but
the triumph over it. The brave man is not he who
does not feel afraid, but he who conquers that fear.*
—NELSON MANDELA

*Do not fear death, but rather the unlived life.
You don't have to live forever, you just have to live.*
—NATALIE BABBITT

THE SPARK THAT CATALYZED MY JOURNEY toward confronting my
fears came from a conversation in 2019. At that time,
I had made a brief appearance in a documentary en-
titled *Game Changers*, which focused on athletes and
plant-based diets. This experience opened doors for
me, connecting me with a vibrant community of like-
minded individuals.

Among them was a woman who was deeply passionate about animal rights activism. As she shared
her stories and showed me pictures from her travels,
I couldn't help but notice the recurring theme that
she often ventured into the world alone. The thought
of her traveling solo to various corners of the globe
sent a rush of anxiety through me. My hands grew
clammy, butterflies danced in my stomach, and I
could feel my heart racing.

I had traveled internationally many times before,

but never on my own. The idea of embarking on such a journey solo was both exhilarating and terrifying. I knew that growth often comes from stepping into discomfort, so I decided to embrace this. That offseason, I made up my mind: I would confront my fears and try traveling alone.

A major breakthrough in addressing my fears came when I decided to learn to surf. I'd see pictures of surfers in barrels and imagine how magical it'd be. I wanted to learn, but I was afraid of the ocean—rip currents, sharks, stingrays, jellyfish. And it was drilled in our heads through movies that sharks were people-eaters.

In order to ride a barrel, I'd have to get comfortable hanging where I couldn't touch. So during the pandemic I found a surf camp in Bahia, Brazil. We weren't allowed to be close to other people but we could be outside. The camp was located right on the beach and hosted by an ex-professional and Brazilian, Beto Diaz. Beto is the *man*—humble, kind, and obsessed with surfing. He harped on the fundamentals. Wanting us to learn how to paddle and get up on our own. He wasn't one of the instructors who was going to push you into a wave. He wanted us to learn the skills so that we could apply them wherever else we decided to ride.

On the third day, with two sessions per day, I finally stood up on my board. It wasn't pretty but I was up and riding a wave—cheesing ear to ear. If you follow me on Instagram you might've seen the video.

No question, surfing and golfing are the two hardest sports I've learned. There are so many factors that come with catching a wave. The first is the ocean, it's always changing and no wave is ever the same. Then there's paddling. I have a strong back and core, but paddling efficiently is another beast. And then you need to have the flexibility and stability to pop up and stand. All the while reading the wave, directing the board, and having proper timing. Not to mention watching out for other surfers and the danger of potential sea life.

I was frustrated but determined, and I journaled about some of my successes. Here's an example:

March 2021
Yesterday I was able to stand on a couple waves. The coolest part was Beto being there to high-five me at the end. I can say that I somewhat conquered my fear of being far out in the ocean. Not fully conquered until I can hang out alone in the water. But I can say that I'm proud of myself. For standing on the board, for being out in deep water, for not giving up. It is so beautiful here. When it's sunny and when it rains. The palm trees and green surrounding the place. Outdoor seating with tiki coverage. Hammocks everywhere. Would love to have something like this of my own someday. Hosting people, connecting, learning languages. Sharing recipes. Being humans.
I Kenny Stills am a prolific surfer
I Kenny Stills am a prolific surfer

I Kenny Stills am a prolific surfer
I Kenny Stills am a prolific surfer
I Kenny Stills am a prolific surfer
I Kenny Stills am a prolific surfer
I Kenny Stills am a prolific surfer
I Kenny Stills am a prolific surfer
I Kenny Stills am a prolific surfer
I Kenny Stills am a prolific surfer

When I read this now, I think about my process of learning self-love. Before, giving myself props on something so "little" wouldn't have been an option. I would've been frustrated with myself or embarrassed that I was struggling, only recognizing the "big" feats.

Since March of 2021, I've spent more time in the ocean than ever before, sometimes even venturing out beyond the break, alone. Every now and then, my mind drifts to thoughts of sharks and a sense of uneasiness creeps in. I don't know if that fear will ever truly go away, but what I choose to focus on is the feeling of the water, the rush of catching a wave, the connection to nature, the exercise, and the community that comes with it.

It all comes down to where I direct my energy. If I focus on the risks, on what could go wrong, of course I'll panic. But the more I put myself in those situations, the easier it gets. I've learned that fear doesn't always disappear, but it becomes manageable. I remind myself of the saying, *Do what you fear, and the fear disappears.* The more I face it, the easier it becomes to push through. When anxiety creeps in,

I pause, take a breath, and center myself. But sometimes, despite all my preparation, I panic, paddle back in, and reset. And that's okay too.

That particular shift in mindset began back in 2019. It pushed me to face my fears head-on and reframe them as challenges, not obstacles. Since then, I've thrown myself into experiences that once intimidated me—skydiving, bungee jumping, parasailing, even getting scuba-certified and volunteering to speak at events. It's more than just seeking thrills or danger. It's proving to myself that I can handle whatever challenges are thrown my way.

In the end, we only regret the chances we *didn't* take.

I GET OUT

Knowin' my condition is the reason I must change
Your stinkin' resolution is no type of solution
Preventin' me from freedom, maintainin' your pollution
I won't support your lie no more, I won't even try no more
If I have to die, oh Lord, that's how I choose to live
—LAURYN HILL

ALTHOUGH I KNEW IN MY HEAD that I was done with football,
I didn't yet feel the need to formally retire. I wasn't
ready to celebrate my career or have others celebrate
it for me. It wasn't about the end of the game, it was
the weight of what would come next that felt overwhelming. The pressure to have some grand plan or
clear next step. Maybe eventually I'll use this as a reason to gather people and reflect, but in that moment I
just needed space to breathe before jumping into the
expectations of the next chapter.

From 2016 to 2019, the protest was seen as a nuisance.
We were vilified, dismissed, and condemned for standing up against injustice. Fans, players, team owners, and
even the US president himself spoke out against us.
But then, in 2020, everything changed. After the murder of George Floyd and the release of a collaborative
video by a group of players asking, "What if I were
George Floyd?" the NFL suddenly shifted its tone.

Commissioner Roger Goodell responded with a statement:

> *We, the National Football League, condemn racism and the systematic oppression of Black people. We, the National Football League, admit we were wrong for not listening to NFL players earlier and encourage all to speak out and peacefully protest. We, the National Football League, believe Black Lives Matter.*

It was a nice response, one that sounded sincere on the surface. But let's be real: by 2020, their back was against the wall. They couldn't ignore the pressure any longer. I later found out that the video was posted to the NFL's social media without the league's approval. Whoever executed that, props to you for making it happen.

But here's the thing. Just because they changed their tone doesn't mean they changed their beliefs. The NFL was forced to make a statement, but did it come from a place of true understanding and commitment? Or was it a calculated move to save face? The weight of everything else—the years of silence, the lack of real support when we needed it—now sits alongside their "new" stance. And that makes their change feel less like progress and more like damage control.

Commissioner Goodell publicly acknowledged the NFL's mistakes, admitting they hadn't handled the protests well and pledging to do better. But I never heard from him personally. Did I expect to? Absolutely not. Still, it's hard to ignore how disingenuous that statement felt. It wasn't like he had a long list of players to reach out to.

I didn't realize it at the time, but I see it clearly now and I have no shame in admitting it: I was hurt. We'd tried to do the "right thing," and it felt like we were left out to dry because of it. The narrative being told not only affected public perception, but also impacted relationships and business partnerships, and derailed careers.

And the impact didn't stop with me. It rippled out to my parents and my family, affecting their work and their relationships as well.

As someone who's always been sensitive, and who has leaned deeper into emotional fluency through therapy, I began to better understand what I needed. In that moment, it wasn't praise for what I'd done, it was acknowledgment of what I'd been through.

We often say, *Football is family.* We talk about brotherhood, about protecting the shield. But that's not how it felt going through all of this. What I wanted was reconciliation. But I had to come to terms with a hard truth: no matter what the tagline says, this is still a business. And business doesn't always make space for healing.

Eventually, I did get a call from Troy Vincent, the NFL's executive vice president of football operations. But it wasn't the kind of conversation I'd been hoping for. Instead of something heartfelt, it felt scripted, the kind of generic apology you've probably heard before: *If we ever did anything to hurt you, we're sorry . . .*

It didn't feel connected. And the truth is, I had to ask for it. I could tell he hadn't really put himself in our shoes and didn't fully grasp what we had gone through. I don't hold that against him, or anyone for that matter, but it was something I noticed.

Now that the NFL's stance had changed, they wanted to work together. But I was skeptical. And still grappling with the painful truth, the truth about how deep systemic oppression runs and how many people are complicit in upholding it.

When George Floyd was murdered, many wounds reopened. Pain left me bedridden for days. I'd had this mistaken feeling of hope and progress completely obliterated.

I remember seeing the video first and not really processing it. I was disturbed but desensitized. It wasn't until the next day, while reading *I'm Still Here: Black Dignity in a World Made for Whiteness* by Austin Channing Brown, that a chord was struck. I bawled, and in that moment I took a picture of myself. I wanted to remember this pain. I'd let the accolades and the illusion of progress blind me, and I promised myself I would never let that happen again.

As soon as the protest began, it felt like I was walking through a tidal wave, fighting against a powerful force, with everything stacked against us. So when the Players Association proposed collaborating on a T-shirt for the season opener, I was cautious. On the surface, it seemed like a gesture of solidarity, but deep down I sensed it was more about optics. I felt that in the end this was a feel-good play—they wanted to make me feel involved but not execute anything with real substance.

When it came down to making the T-shirt, I was supposed to give them ideas for approval. Of course, they didn't like what I sent over. In the end, what they wanted was permission to use a caption from my Instagram: *If they come for one of us, they come for all of us.* I gave them permission and asked not to be included in the release in any way, and moved on.

The design I had proposed for the T-shirt was, *AM I NEXT?* A question I thought was more than fitting. The league is majority Black and police brutality disproportionately affects our communities. The shirt was a reflection of that harsh reality. Like any other shirt the league hands out, wearing it wouldn't be mandatory, but I believed it carried the weight of something important. I also felt it aligned with the video the players had put out earlier: *We Are All George Floyd.* It shouldn't require someone's death for action to finally be taken.

The more I paid attention, the more frustrated I became with the league for not using its power to control the narrative. As I grew and evolved, I started seeing things for what they really were. The more work I did on my emotional intelligence and feelings of self-worth, the more I realized that being in NFL buildings just didn't feel right anymore. I was working so hard to be the truest version of myself, trying to eliminate negativity, drama, and everything fake from my life. The corporate world and the locker room no longer aligned with who I was becoming.

By my last year in 2021, back with the Saints, I'd lost my spark. No matter how hard I tried to hype myself up, game day didn't excite me the way it once had. The lights would come on, and where I used to show out, now I'd drop the ball, literally. National TV spots turned into my worst performances. I hadn't changed my preparation, but my game was falling flat. My views had shifted. The logical side of my brain began to take over, and the "whatever it takes" attitude I once lived by was no longer there. What had once felt like a necessary drive now seemed out of sync.

Maybe it was just in my head, but I had a growing sense that I wasn't wanted. In Houston in 2020, it felt like they'd kept me on the sidelines on purpose. I was still in my prime, earning good money—but riding the bench. I even asked for a trade, seeing the writing on the wall. But with wide receivers Will Fuller and Brandin Cooks dealing with injuries, they kept me around.

Later that year, I signed with Buffalo for the playoffs. When I arrived and got to work, they were surprised that I still "had it," which told me exactly what rumors the Texans had been spreading.

When I eventually signed with the Saints in 2021, I didn't have many options. And they reached out only because of familiarity. I don't want to say the league was actively keeping me out, but it sure felt that way. After years of playing at a high level and no major injuries, I couldn't buy into the idea that I was suddenly "done."

The politics didn't help my motivation either. When I rejoined the Saints, the staff asked me not to take a knee during the anthem, despite the league printing and promoting *End Racism* and *It Takes All of Us* on the fields. They were profiting off these causes while still silencing voices like mine. We agreed I'd sit on the bench during the anthem, and if you find pictures from that season, you'll see me doing just that. Honestly, this was my last chance, and my patience was thin. I'd stuck around out of respect for mentors who encouraged me, but deep down I no longer wanted to be part of an environment that felt so hypocritical.

In the end, it was my play that got me released, but I have to say, the parting was mutual. I was there out of respect for the talent I had. I couldn't shake the guilt of knowing I had more to give and that I was letting it go to waste.

I spent twenty-five years playing football, missing only one season when I broke my ankle at age twelve. The game taught me lessons that go far beyond the field. Lessons that I now carry into the next chapter of my life. Discipline, attention to detail, punctuality, leadership, teamwork, the ability to adapt on the fly, and the capacity to handle high-pressure situations and criticism. And I know that each of these qualities is just as valuable off the field as they were on it.

What I have to remember now is the mindset that helped me reach the top in the first place. The attitude, the effort, the grind. I've already proven I can achieve greatness, and that same drive will carry me to new heights once again.

ATHLETES FOR CEASEFIRE

Goodness is a choice:
  Stopping yourself from doing what's wrong is not the same as choosing what's right and doing it. Don't stand on the verge of being good. Be as good as you can be. If you can give, give.
  If you can help, help.
  If you can make someone's day by a simple act of kindness, make it.
  Set the bar of success for yourself as high as the best that you can be, not as low as avoiding the worst that you can be.
                    —AUTHOR UNKNOWN

The NBA and NBPA mourn the horrific loss of life in Israel and condemn these acts of terrorism. We stand with the people of Israel and pray for peace for the entire region.
  —JOINT STATEMENT BY THE NBA AND NBPA

The NFL mourns the loss of innocent lives in Israel and strongly condemns all forms of terrorism. The depravity of these acts is beyond comprehension, and we grieve with the families of those killed, in-

jured, and still missing. We pray for peace and will
always stand against the evils of hate.
          —OFFICIAL STATEMENT FROM THE NFL

IN 2024, OMAR DREIDI AND I LAUNCHED Athletes for Ceasefire with the goal of raising awareness and providing educational resources about the ongoing situation in Gaza.

Omar was in Palestine when the events of October 7 unfolded. We exchanged many calls during that period, and when he returned to the US, we met in Los Angeles. I immediately felt the need to act, to organize, and to speak out.

Our first step was to reach out to activists, media personalities, and athletes who were already vocal about Palestine. We were fortunate to engage people like Dr. Angela Davis, Palestinian American scholar and activist Noura Erakat, and Marc Lamont Hill, among others. These are some of the most respected civil rights and Palestinian activists and they quickly recognized the intention behind Athletes for Ceasefire. They shared our belief in the potential for athletes to affect meaningful change.

Our goal was to enlist a few high-profile athletes from every sport, hoping that their involvement would create a ripple effect and encourage others to sign onto our ceasefire letter. But enlisting athletes proved harder than expected. We reached out to NBA head coaches like Gregg Popovich and Steve Kerr, sending emails, texts, and direct messages to everyone within reach. Yet many athletes were intimidated.

In order to support athletes who wanted to speak out, Omar held a meeting with the National Basketball Players Association (NBPA) to try to provide a safety net for NBA athletes who chose to sign the letter or otherwise show solidarity with Palestine. His request was ignored, leaving athletes to face potential repercussions alone.

In a private Zoom meeting, several athletes voiced their fears of backlash and losing jobs, sponsorships, and valuable connections. Omar and I understood their apprehension. We'd seen how the NBA treated Kyrie Irving after he shared a link to a film alleged to contain anti-Semitic themes. His suspension without pay and the requirements for his return were, to many, an excessive response. Also, some felt that the involvement of the Anti-Defamation League (ADL) was problematic due to their political orientation.

These instances underscore a harsh reality about free speech and the consequences of questioning narratives surrounding Israel. When speaking out invites personal and professional backlash, it raises important questions: If challenging the status quo leads to punishment, what does that reveal about the system itself? Doesn't this response confirm concerns about the imbalance of power?

The situation in Gaza is increasingly heartbreaking. The mounting death toll, especially among innocent children, along with the bombing of hospitals and schools, have become unbearable realities that flood social media in real time. Yet the fear of being labeled anti-Semitic discourages many from voicing their concerns about Israel's actions, keeping necessary dialogue suppressed.

To date, over 350 athletes from across sports have courageously signed our letter supporting a ceasefire. Their willingness to stand up for humanity reflects a conviction that empathy, peace, and justice must be prioritized. However, the absence of high-profile, active players is hard to ignore.

Athletes have historically been powerful advocates for change, and now, more than ever, we need engaged, conscious voices willing to lead. Today's young people wield tremendous influence, but it's worth asking: what are they truly standing for? Beyond brand deals, there's a growing opportunity to balance visibility with genuine civic engagement, compassion, and meaningful action. When athletes step up for causes that matter, they do more than lend their fame; they become a force for justice, inspiring others to believe that, even in a divided world, humanity can come first.

EMBRACING CHANGE

Embarrassment is the cost of entry. If you aren't willing to look like a foolish beginner, you'll never become a graceful master.
—ED LATIMORE

Jobs fill your pocket, adventures fill your soul.
—JAIME LYN BEATTY

WITH THE END ALWAYS IN MIND, I strived to keep myself sharp. I took online courses and went to business conferences. I was passionate about other professions but I didn't know exactly what I wanted to do. I knew that I loved to travel, that I was interested in clothing design, scriptwriting, and acting, and I considered becoming an entrepreneur.

But I also thought about the wealth of knowledge I'd acquired around the game of football. I knew I wanted to help the next generation, but I also didn't want to coach. I saw their schedules and lifestyle and knew it wasn't for me. If I was going to continue to be in the building at that capacity, then I might as well still be playing.

Although I had been preparing for the end of my football career, facing it still made me anxious. I'd never fully identified as "Kenny Stills, football player." When I'd meet someone new, work would be the last thing I'd bring up. I wanted people to know me beyond the field—but who was I without it? This curiosity, mixed with a little uncertainty about what the future held, made me realize I had one option: to lean in and find out.

In 2020, after my release from the Texans, I had discovered a newfound passion for snowboarding. I had visited Aspen, Colorado, and instantly knew this was a place I might want to settle once it was all over.

That year in Aspen, I had my first snowboarding lesson. Growing up, I'd ridden a few times, but getting instruction changed everything. Suddenly, I understood the curvature of the board and how to use my athleticism and strength to control the ride. Finding a new hobby to immerse myself in made the transition feel much smoother. I spent my days in a different environment, learning new skills and connecting with like-minded people.

Even though I grew obsessed with this new passion after I left the NFL, there were still moments when I'd come home from riding and feel anxious, as if there was something more important I should be doing. All I'd ever known was the grind. Letting go of that mindset, learning to find joy in just living, was going to be a process.

I hadn't explained to anyone what I was doing. My dad would text about job openings—playing and coaching. I'd get texts from former teammates about training together and the occasional call from my agent about interest from NFL teams. But for me, football was in the past.

To help with the anxiety, I started to journal about future goals and what I wanted to accomplish. I put together a one-pager, showing who I was and what I stood for. But I couldn't help wondering: *How am I going to find a job that aligns with my passions and also connects me with the kind of people I want to be around?* I wasn't about to leave the NFL's corporate environment only to jump into another one that didn't fit who I was becoming.

First I had to learn to live. Being okay with the simple things: waking up in the morning, making breakfast, working out, doing life admin. I had to learn to manage my time, figure out what relationships to nourish, and discover what truly brought me joy. Early on, I said yes to everything. Music festival, last-minute trip to Monaco to see Formula One, spiritual journey to India—it was now time for me to do anything and everything I never even imagined.

In 2015, I met a lovely man named Ganesh at a restaurant in Carlsbad, California. My first two offseasons I would head home to get out of Louisiana, train, and be close to Mom. She had a connection for a timeshare close to the beach and it was right around the corner from an Exos training facility. Which worked out perfectly.

One evening, Mike Hodges and I stepped out to grab a bite. (To refresh your memory, Mike joined me on the road trip.) At the bar, this guy caught my attention—loud, laughing, living it up in a way that felt rare. Most of the drunk folks I'd been around ended up angry or looking for a fight, but this guy was different. His face lit up with a smile and he was talking to everyone around him like they were old friends. Naturally, I was intrigued. Eventually, he struck up a conversation with us and we hit it off. I could tell right away that he had a big heart—and the best part? He had no idea I played football; he didn't know a thing about me. That was refreshing. He made such an impression that we exchanged numbers. I knew I wanted to hang out with this guy again, sober.

Next time we met up, Ganesh invited me to his home for a traditional Indian meal. I'd never had one before, and honestly, never had an Indian homie either. At his place, his mom and wife laid out a spread of mostly Southern India cuisine. We ate with our hands, yogurt on standby to cool the spice. Afterward, we sat back and watched cricket highlights, a whole new world. I didn't know a thing about the sport, had no idea the matches could last days, or that players had cultlike followings. The meal was full of flavors I'd never experienced, and from that night on I was all about exploring more of their culture.

Not long after meeting Ganesh, I was traded to the Miami Dolphins. For the next eight years, we kept in touch through texts and Facebook, but life got in the way and we never had the chance to reconnect in person. Then, out of the blue in May 2023, I got a message from G. He asked if I happened to be in San Diego and wanted to grab lunch. By chance I was, but I was leaving for Europe the next day and had a list of last-minute errands to tackle. Still, I dropped everything to go see my guy and his family.

As we caught up, his wife, Sowmi, mentioned that he'd be traveling across India for the entire month of July and suggested I join him. I checked my calendar, saw I had no major plans, and told him I was in. That evening, once Ganesh sent over his flight info, my ticket was booked: Miami to Chennai. We'd spend July road-tripping through India, visiting temples and connecting to the source.

I had seen bits of India in films and read about its layers of society in the book *Caste* by Isabel Wilkerson, but I kept my mind open, choosing not to make assumptions or hold expectations. I'd heard about the intense smells and immense poverty, and many people warned me I might get sick. But none of that phased me. I had Ganesh with me, what could go wrong?

We would be joined on the trip by another young man by the name of Gavyn. He was on the self-discovery path, and had previously volunteered with Ganesh's organization, Bloom to Life. Bloom to Life is a US-based nonprofit that contributes financial assistance to surgeries pertaining to congenital heart disease in India—where a quarter of a million babies die each year due to lack of care. Along with our spiritual journey, we'd visit the hospital and meet with the extraordinary staff that Bloom to Life supports.

I landed in Chennai on July 2, greeted by Ganesh's warm energy and contagious smile. Over the next two weeks we traveled from the east coast of India to the southernmost tip, then back up the west coast, making our way to Kerala. We visited many Hindu temples along the way—who knew India boasted over six hundred thousand temples? When visiting the temples I practiced as a Hindu would, keeping proper etiquette—barefoot, in a dhoti, and shirtless when it was called for. All the while doing my best to remember to accept and give offerings with the right hand, being that the left is considered impure.

In my prayers and meditations, I gave thanks for my circumstances—my health and relationships—and asked for continued guidance and direction in my life. I asked that the spirits watch over my loved ones and bring us all closer together, and I gave thanks in advance that their will would be done.

One of my favorite memories was the night of Girivalam (pronounced *Gi-ri-va-lum*). Girivalam is a Hindu practice held in Tiruvannamalai (pronounced *Tee-roo-vuhn-nuh-muh-lie*) where devotees walk barefoot around the foothills of Arunachala Hill under the full moon. Ganesh and I joined in, covering eight miles, visiting sacred lingams along the way. Walking barefoot felt like a mark of respect, and the ritual itself is said to purify the mind and body, bringing spiritual liberation and divine blessings. Over our four-hour journey, we had plenty of time to catch up on everything we'd missed over the past eight years. Work, family, politics, you name it. Somewhere along that trek, Ganesh shared the story behind Bloom to Life and why he was so passionate about it.

In short, US government aid made a difference for Ganesh's family, helping with the birth of his second child. That experience flipped a switch for him, showing how powerless people can feel when finances hold them back from giving their kids a fighting chance. Seeing that struggle and the health crisis spreading in India, Ganesh founded Bloom to Life to save as many children as possible.

Since its start in 2015, Bloom to Life has helped save over 150 lives through Amrita Hospital in Kerala. Visiting this hospital touched my heart in ways I didn't expect. The team worked tirelessly to heal these children and support their families. They walked me through the intricacies of their preparation, using technology like 3D printing and virtual reality to handle complex surgeries. They even allowed me to observe a heart surgery up close. Watching a heart beat, pump, and sustain life, then stop for the team to get to work, was surreal. I felt privileged just being there, witnessing the miracles they make happen.

Every day at that hospital, tears filled my eyes. Seeing people come together for a cause greater than themselves filled me with optimism. There was no hierarchy, just a team of highly skilled individuals working with minimal resources, giving everything they had to make a difference. What struck me most was that everything was done at cost, with no expectation of profit, driven solely by a commitment to care. These men and women sacrificed personal comfort to give others a chance. They quickly became my heroes, not just for their sacrifices but for the community they built. In that hospital, everyone felt appreciated, supported, and driven to do their best for each other.

After visiting Amrita, I knew exactly where I'd want my loved ones cared for in a cardiac emergency. To show my support, I made a donation to Bloom to Life in honor of each of my seven siblings.

Even as I stood up against racism, discrimination, and oppression in the US, I couldn't escape my own prejudice toward one particular group. I was only nine years old when the Twin Towers were attacked on September 11, 2001. In the wake of that tragedy, the country came together in a wave of nationalism and patriotism, united by grief and anger. But in that collective response, I unknowingly internalized a narrative that linked Muslims, Arabs, and the whole Middle East with terrorism. The media fueled this perception, painting these groups as violent and extremist, and I, like many others, was caught up in that narrative. I felt both frightened and offended by those who wore hijabs or head wraps, convinced that they were somehow a threat. The stories we were told painted them as enemies of America, people who sought to destroy everything we stood for, believing they were promised rewards in the afterlife for committing acts of terror.

When I visited my first Muslim-majority country in February 2020, my prejudice resurfaced. Alone in

Marrakech, Morocco, I was surrounded by people wearing hijabs and heard prayer calls echoing over loudspeakers. I felt on edge, clutching my belongings and avoiding crowds, convinced that harm could be lurking at any moment.

To better understand the place, I hired a local guide named Mohamed, who quickly became my friend. He was slender, goofy, loved his cigarettes, and always wore a hat that reminded me of Indiana Jones. Over the next few days, we traveled together to the coast and through the Atlas Mountains, exploring the country's beauty and getting to know each other. As our conversations deepened, I realized how wrong I had been. The narrative I had been fed about Muslims was not only misleading, it was dangerously simplistic.

As I spent more time reflecting, the fear I'd held about the hijab and the stereotypes around it began to fade. I questioned the label of "terrorist" and who gets to decide who is called that. It became clear to me that extremism exists in *all* communities, and that my narrow view was rooted in ignorance, not facts.

One of the most eye-opening moments came when we visited Mohamed's family in the small town of Ouarzazate. Their home was humble, and despite the language barrier, I was greeted with an overwhelming sense of warmth. They prepared a Thanksgiving-style feast and I ate as much as I could, aware that not finishing everything might be seen as disrespectful. It was an impossible task. In the end, I found myself in a food coma, sprawled out on the floor with my hands resting on my full stomach.

Mohamed's mother and sister wore full hijabs, and at first the cultural differences felt awkward. I instinctively wanted to express my appreciation with a handshake or a hug, but quickly realized that wasn't appropriate. So I bowed and offered as many thanks as I could before we headed out.

It was during this trip that I finally let go of my prejudice. I realized that all people, regardless of their ethnicity or beliefs, can be pushed to extremes—but that doesn't define them. I began to understand that instead of focusing on labels and assumptions, we should ask ourselves what has happened to certain people to lead them in destructive directions in the first place. This experience didn't just change my views about Muslims, it changed my understanding of *humanity*, and I left Morocco with a new sense of openness and a commitment to challenge the stereotypes I once held.

TÍO GOPHER: A LEGACY OF PRIDE, RESISTANCE, AND REFLECTION

A CENTRAL THEME IN MY PERSONAL JOURNEY has been connecting to my roots. My passion for activism sparked an early dive into African and African American history—books, documentaries, and museums. From there, I took the next step in exploring my heritage, starting with an African ancestry test that traced my roots back to Gabon. Yet, while I learned much about my African heritage, I had neglected the other side of my family, my Mexican roots.

Growing up, I felt embarrassed by my Mexican heritage. Mexicans were often painted as dirty, poor, or dumb, and associated with stereotypes about field-work, "illegals," and cartels. As a biracial person, it felt like I had to choose a side. Was I Mexican or was I Black?

In school, I wasn't Mexican enough to belong to the Mexican crowd, especially since I barely spoke Spanish. And I wasn't Black enough to belong in the Black crowd either. I was often called "yellow boy," "light bright," "mixed breed," or "chico." None of that really offended me, just reminded me that I was different.

Unconsciously trying to assimilate, my mom only spoke Spanish to me when I was in trouble. I knew the bad words and I caught on to others by hearing her gossip on the phone with Grandma. Anything she didn't want us to know she'd say in Spanish.

It wasn't until I took a deeper dive into Black history that I realized how much I had neglected my Mexican side, and why. I thought back to my childhood, embarrassed that I was Mexican. I couldn't stand roll call. People knew me as Kenny Stills, not Kenneth Stills or Kenneth Lee de la O Stills. "Delgado, who's that?" As soon as I heard *Kenneth*, I'd try to speak up to avoid the humiliation of the mispronunciation.

When we visited Mexico for my mom's sixtieth birthday, I began to reconnect with this heritage. We explored Mexico City and San Miguel de Allende, learning about ancient civilizations, tasting traditional foods, visiting the house of Frida Kahlo, and celebrating Día de los Muertos. It filled me with pride as I realized how deeply connected we are to this land, its rich history and traditions. It became clear to me how foolish I had been to ever feel ashamed.

A major influence on my newfound pride was my great-uncle, Tío Gilbert. Born in New Ulm, Minnesota in 1945, he was a community leader, activist, Vietnam War veteran, and Purple Heart recipient. Much like me, Tío struggled with feeling proud of his Mexican heritage, growing up in an era when Mexicans were typecast as either gardeners or criminals. He experienced firsthand the humiliation of having his sisters' names changed in school, the punishment for speaking Spanish, and the systemic discrimination Mexican Americans faced in the '50s and '60s. This frustration led him to a period of rebellion. Tío described how he and his peers responded to discrimination by becoming "tough guys," retaliating against those who mocked them. This aggression led to a stint in jail for a drive-by-shooting incident. But through the support of an organization called Neighborhood House, he was able to redirect his life and eventually serve his country in the Vietnam War.

Tío was always searching for a sense of purpose, and the military gave him the structure and respect he had been missing. But his perspective on war shifted dramatically after he saw the *Hearts and Minds* documentary, in which a Vietnamese man mourns the loss of his daughter. The pain he saw in that man's eyes led Tío to reevaluate his views on violence, making him a lifelong proponent of peace and reconciliation. His change of heart became a cornerstone of his activism in the Chicano movement. He worked tirelessly to establish Chicano Studies at the University of Minnesota, advocated for migrant workers, and helped build cultural pride. He was a member of the Brown Berets and worked alongside Cesar Chavez to support the Mexican American labor movement. His activism didn't stop there; he continued to serve his community, working at Neighborhood House, offering support to marginalized families, and ensuring that the doors of opportunity were open for future generations.

Through Tío, I learned the importance of connecting with my heritage, of fighting for justice, and of the power of reconciliation. Tío was the first person to speak openly to me about the concept of healing in this way. He shared how his experiences in Vietnam changed his life and how that transformation shaped his work for the community.

Tío passed away in August 2021, after his second battle with cancer. But his final thoughts, shared in an interview, stayed with me: "People need to know what has gone before and how they benefit from the work of others. Things that we take for granted today—translators in hospitals, courts, and schools—were hard-won victories. We fought for these opportunities so that you could step through the doors. Remember, you're standing on our shoulders."

Growing up far from my family, we lost touch with many traditions. My sisters stayed in Minnesota with my grandmother, and my brother returned there when he was seventeen. It was just my mom and me in California, and with that came sacrifice. We were disconnected from our blood and our roots. Yet Tío kept the connection alive, visiting me in Florida and supporting me when I got involved in protests and activism. Even in his final years, he encouraged me to keep fighting the good fight. I like to think that our shared passion for justice and change was rooted in our blood, a legacy passed down through generations of struggle and triumph.

By reconnecting with my Mexican heritage and

absorbing the legacy of Tío Gilbert, I learned to embrace *all* parts of who I am. Tío's story is a reminder that we all have a role to play in shaping the world around us. We stand on the shoulders of those who came before, and it's up to us to pass on the wisdom, strength, and pride that was gifted to us.

PSYCHEDELICS AND OTHER
MIND-ALTERING SUBSTANCES

Whatever is fluid, soft, and yielding
will overcome whatever is rigid and hard.
What is soft is strong.
—Lao Tzu

My interest in psychedelics began in high school when I learned that humans don't use the full capacity of our brains. And as research on brain injuries evolved, I started exploring regenerative medicine. My dad played defense in the 1980s, when football was much more brutal, and I've had my own share of concussions. Seeing players take their lives and donate their brains for study made me start to question our future. If cannabis, as plant medicine, had given me relief all of those years, what else was out there and how could it potentially help?

Through recreational use, and later as I became an advocate for psychedelics, I met countless people whose lives have been transformed by plant medicines. Psilocybin mushrooms, for example, have roots in ancient practices and have long been used in spiritual ceremonies by indigenous peoples. So what's the hold-up in the Western world? Among other reasons, we're up against stigma, the "war on drugs," and the international ban of 1971.

The "war on drugs" significantly impacted the direction of psychedelics, with smear campaigns, research suppression, and legal restrictions. People had been scared into linking psychedelics to the countercultural hippie movement, and the risks have been exaggerated, including reports that they lead to insanity or chromosome damage. Because of this, it became less respectable for scientists to study psychedelics, and over time research was halted and the findings lost or destroyed.

As of late, however, there has been a resurgence in research and the recreational use of psychedelics. Psilocybin, MDMA, ketamine, and LSD are all being used for research and therapy, with promising results. This is one area where activism and the mental health space meet.

Recently, I had the opportunity to spend time with a couple folks from the veteran community. One man's story in particular became etched in my brain.

Once a proud Navy SEAL, Punky had endured unimaginable trials. Haunted by the shadows of his past, including sexual and physical abuse, he fought to prove himself in the armed forces. But the joy of achievement was short-lived; he lost friends almost immediately to the brutalities of war. Sadness engulfed him, yet he felt unable to truly grieve, burying his emotions beneath the chaos of combat.

War became his outlet, but it also led him to spiral into addiction. Drugs and alcohol dulled his pain, leading to a divorce and the loss of custody of his children. In the depths of his despair, deployment felt like the only escape, a way to numb his torment and memories. As the weight of his struggles grew heavier, Punky found himself on the brink of suicide. One fateful night, gun in hand, he was ready to end it all when the doorbell rang. It was a friend he'd been helping, a familiar face who sensed something was terribly wrong. That simple act of connection became a turning point. His friend introduced him to psychedelic-assisted therapy, a concept Punky was skeptical about. But as he listened to others in this community share their experiences, he began to see he wasn't alone in his suffering. Some of them had faced similar demons and had emerged with hope.

Deciding to give it a chance, Punky tried ibogaine, a natural psychoactive substance found in plants from West Africa and traditionally used in spiritual rituals. The experience was transformative, taking him back to his childhood where he could confront pain he had long buried, guiding him through a journey of healing and reconciliation. He came to understand not just the horrors he faced but also how to forgive those who had wronged him and, most importantly, to forgive himself.

What felt like years of therapy unfolded in one night, reshaping his life. Now, Punky stands as an advocate for others like him, helping veterans find the support and healing they desperately need. His path from despair to hope ignites a light in those still struggling, proving that even in the darkest moments, change is possible.

* * *

Punky's story isn't unique; countless men and women have turned to sacred plant medicines to find healing and gain perspective. But the stigma around these medicines often blocks us from getting the help we need. In my view, this stigma is fueled by the pharmaceutical industry. If more people used natural and homeopathic treatments, the industry wouldn't be quite as profitable. Still profitable, sure, but not at the level they are now. The US system often puts profit over people, and it's easy to see when you look at the high costs of healthy food, quality education, and reputable health care.

I'm not sharing my experiences with plant medicines to advocate for any one path, but rather to open up the possibility that alternatives exist. Over the years, I've explored many mind-altering substances, but for the sake of this book, I'll focus on the ones that undoubtedly shaped my journey.

I've used cannabis since I was fourteen. To this day, it lightens my mood, relieves pain, and helps with creativity. Over the years, I've had this internal battle with how serious I see things. When I'm in a funk, smoking gets me out of my head, and helps me to chat and make jokes and see the brighter side. Over time, I've built up a tolerance—I can get high and hang out or I can get high and exercise. I'm a functional stoner. Some people smoke cigarettes, drink alcohol or caffeine—I smoke weed.

The first time I remember smelling ganja was when I was ten. Those with siblings know—little brother always tags along with big bro. My brother Lance was five years older and a sophomore in high school. One summer afternoon, we went to his friend's house. They all headed out back and told me to stay on the couch in the living room. I noticed a smell but didn't think anything of it. My parents burned incense all throughout my childhood and this didn't seem too far off. Later on, when we returned home, my mom confronted him. His eyes were red and his clothes reeked, and nothing got past her. I remember Lance wondering what the big deal was. Apparently he'd found my dad's stash at some point. How could they be mad at him if they were doing it too?

As I mentioned earlier, the first time I had weed in my possession, I was twelve and wanted to be cool. Holding onto the weed but not really planning to smoke it. I've said it before but I grew up fast. Sixth grade is when things started coming together for me. I was obsessed with girls and they finally started paying attention to me. At middle school orientation, an eighth grader introduced herself and gave me a picture with her number on the back. It seemed almost immediately I was in with the older crowd. We'd hang out in the hallways between periods talking to girls and passing notes.

In high school, I smoked cannabis whenever I could. My mom didn't approve, and since it was still illegal, we kept it low-key. But I never felt like I was doing anything wrong. The only downside was a hit to my lung capacity, and I could work around that.

Cannabis is natural and offers real health benefits, so its legality didn't mean much to me. Back then, we mostly smoked out of bongs and bowls; I don't know if that was to conserve or the fact that none of us knew how to roll. Most kids kept a piece in their car, sneaking a smoke during class breaks or packing a quick bowl after school. We'd smoke, get the munchies, then watch YouTube, play video games, or turn on a show. It was simple, harmless fun.

Keep in mind, I played sports year-round, so my free time was limited. Smoking was just something I enjoyed on the side, it was never the main focus. I knew to keep my priorities straight but I also made time to enjoy myself. Personal responsibility and accountability were always front and center. I knew that if my grades or athletic performance slipped, all the extra stuff would come to an end.

When I got to the University of Oklahoma, I wanted to keep smoking but Coach Stoops wasn't having it. He tested us often and was quick to suspend anyone he caught. Despite his efforts, most of the time I took the risk. I did some Internet research and found a formula to help me pass the drug tests. Turns out, diluted urine didn't count as a fail, so I'd drink a detox beverage, down a gallon of water, and hit the bathroom as many times as I could before I had to test. Who knows how many times I promised God I'd quit smoking if I just passed THIS test.

Through my research, I found out THC sticks to our fat cells. I was keeping my body fat low, but some teammates weren't so lucky. They failed tests and were kicked off the team. Looking back now, it's wild to think that the NFL and NCAA have finally changed their stance on cannabis. We've known for decades about its benefits, so why are they just catching up? I think about all the athletes who've paid the price for these outdated biases. Athletes like Sha'Carri Richardson, Josh Gordon, and Ricky Williams. People's lives and careers that were seriously altered because of a lack of understanding and progressive thinking.

After ganja, the next life-changer for me was MDMA, a form of Ecstasy that brings on powerful emotions, heightened senses, and euphoria. My first time trying a pill was in high school. Every so often, there'd be a teen function downtown, so we'd grab some booze and hop on the train south. I'd already heard about Ecstasy—ironically, through in-school suspension education. I'd seen it in movies, heard about it in music, and it sounded like a good time. I'd also heard the negative rumors, like it would burn holes in your brain or ruin sex for good. People would say, "If you have sex while you're high, it'll never feel the same."

At first, I used Ecstasy as a party booster—to feel the music, keep the energy going, and stay awake on those long benders. But as I got older, I noticed that being high made me want to talk and connect. I'd get vulnerable, telling my partner things I'd been holding in or pulling a friend aside to open up. The emotions would hit me and sometimes I'd release a deep cry.

Before Ecstasy, I was too ashamed to cry, especially in front of others. But with it, I could let go, and I'd welcome the comfort of a hug or a hand on my shoulder as I let it all out. I credit rapper J. Cole for helping me realize it's okay to cry. In an interview he gave in 2011, he talked openly about this and I felt like he'd given me permission. His album *Cole World: The Sideline Story* became huge for me. In the song "Lost Ones," he says, "*And I ain't too proud to tell you that I cry sometimes, I cry sometimes about it.*" That line hit home. I was checking my pride and my ego and hearing someone I admired show me it was okay.

MDMA opened me up to emotions I didn't know I could feel. For so long, the most notable emotion I showed was anger. Fear? That felt weak. Too much joy or love was labeled as gay. I felt trapped. Like a *caged bird*, cue J. Cole. I'd spent years conditioned to keep my emotions in check, but Ecstasy helped me create new pathways, allowing me to feel, to heal, and to finally express what I'd been holding in. Carrying all that weight from the past was heavy. Letting go meant dropping the macho armor. And once I opened up, I felt lighter.

The more I opened up, the less alone I felt. We're all on our own journeys but we share far more experiences than we think. I'd wanted real connections but was afraid to let people get close. Opening up allowed people to know the real me, and in turn brought me closer to myself.

Psilocybin mushrooms were the next plant medicine to push my evolution forward. I still vividly remember my first experience, being immersed in nature and feeling an overwhelming connection to everything around me. Before that, I'd spent time outside, picking flowers, watching clouds, and even occasionally littering without a second thought. I used resources carelessly and didn't fully grasp the impact of my actions. But when the mushrooms hit, something changed. I could feel the energy of every living thing around me. The trees, the plants, they weren't just background scenery anymore; they were vibrant, breathing beings, sustaining us in ways I had never truly understood. For the first time, I grasped the interconnectedness of everything, how life on earth is all part of a delicate web. I realized how fragile our existence is; here we are, on this rock, floating through space, held together only by gravity. My appreciation for the sanctity of life deepened.

Mushrooms also taught me how to sit with discomfort. When I talk to people about psychedelics, many are concerned about "losing control" or "going off the deep end," worrying they might never come back. The idea of the "bad trip" is a common fear. But for me, there's no such thing. I believe psychedelics bring to the surface what's lurking in our subconscious—issues, emotions, or blockages we need to face. Sometimes, they make us confront old patterns we've avoided. Other times, they heighten our senses, allowing us to pick up on energies from the people around us that we normally miss. Either way, there's always a lesson and that's what makes the experience so valuable.

I've got an example that really brings this home.

After my first season in college, I went home for break and got to spend time with my high school buddies. The plan was for all of us to eat a few grams of mushrooms and chill at a friend's house for the night. First mistake—I don't advise anyone to eat a large dose of shrooms at night, in a home. Set and setting are so important. A safe space, during the day, in nature, is highly recommended. As the mushrooms started to hit, I got into my head. We were all hanging, laughing and working through some initial awkwardness. Then something happened that triggered me. It could have been the words, delivery, or just my own sensitivity. But my brain started to tell my body that I wasn't welcomed. I felt out of place.

Instead of hanging around the guys, I stepped away, finding art to gaze into and playing music on my phone. I noticed the comfort I felt away from the group and in reflection realized how I was just feeling everyone else's energy. My mind was telling me that my friends were jealous of the early success I'd had. But where was I getting that from? Just from one comment that was made? That could've spiraled into something terrible. A potential scuffle or me trying to get behind the wheel of a car and leave. Instead, I changed the setting, put on music, and reset my thoughts until I could return to the group. No problem.

Microdosing has become a hot topic lately. A microdose is simply a very small amount of psilocybin, around 0.1 to 0.3 grams. It's typically found in products like gummies, capsules, or chocolates, and it's designed to give you the benefits of the plant without the full psychedelic experience. The idea isn't to "trip" or alter your perception but rather to enhance things like mood, focus, and creativity in a subtle way. You don't get any of the intense visuals or sensory changes that you might expect from a full dose, but you do start to feel more balanced, clear-headed, and present.

For me, it's been another game-changer. Microdosing here and there has helped me feel more grounded and lifted my mood. Although research is still catching up, early studies are showing that microdosing can have very positive benefits. From what I've experienced, it can help you feel more in tune with yourself, manage stress better, and engage more fully with life.

The psychedelic that's had the deepest impact on me is ketamine. "K" is the only federally legal psychedelic in the US. It is a dissociative anesthetic that has some hallucinogenic properties, and is commonly used for treatment of pain and depression.

According to John Krystal, MD, at the Yale School of Medicine, "Ketamine can produce feelings of unreality; visual and sensory distortions; a distorted feeling about one's body; temporary unusual thoughts and beliefs; and a euphoria or a buzz."

I first started using K recreationally in 2016. I enjoyed the disassociation from my thoughts. I immediately felt the ego and self-judgment go out the door. I felt the freedom to explore and be myself and figure out who that is. If Ecstasy helped me to release the weight, ketamine helped to break the chains. For the first time, I wasn't afraid to speak the "weird" things on my mind, or feel the music and dance, or just totally let loose without judgment. I felt free. And realized that freedom was an attitude.

I'm grateful for these medicines for showing me what's available. Helping me to access feelings and emotions I'd locked away since I was a child. The movie *Inside Out* gives a remarkable visual representation of this with "personality islands." The animated film is about an eleven-year-old girl who moves from Minnesota to San Francisco and how her five core emotions—Fear, Anger, Joy, Disgust, and Sadness—struggle to cope with her new life. In the movie, the girl's personality is depicted through these islands: Goofball, Friendship, Hockey, Honesty, and Family. All the islands were created from crucial memories, accumulated through her childhood, and each is powered by a specific core memory.

This film provoked introspection about my own life.

In my house, Goofball Island did not exist. We made jokes and talked shit about other people, but to totally let loose and be goofy was unheard of. Friendship Island constantly fractured as I moved from city to city and school to school. That helped me to make new friends but created a struggle to harness long-lasting, nurturing relationships. Honesty Island was hit with a hurricane at age five when I was told to lie to my mom about my dad and my whereabouts.

And Family Island was damaged many times: When we moved to California, leaving my sisters to live with Grandma. Seeing my parents' on-and-off and sometimes dysfunctional relationship. Having my brother sent off to live with his dad. Going through periods of no communication between siblings and parents. I haven't spoken to one of my brothers since 2021.

Intentionally using substances has helped me tap into certain childlike behaviors. With intention I can explore, then integrate once sober. Using my imagination, having a broad spectrum of emotions, choosing radical honesty, being a goofball. It's such a relief to reconnect with these qualities. It's like rediscovering pieces of myself I didn't even know I'd lost, and it makes me wonder how many other parts of me are waiting to be awakened.

Intention has been key. Now that I know what exists, I don't have to use substances in order to get there. Yes, it's easier to use substances to let loose, but it's not necessary.

Once again, I want to be clear: I'm not here to advocate for drug use, nor am I promoting psychedelics. What I'm sharing is my *own* experience—how these substances have influenced me and the lessons I've learned along the way. I understand that, like anything in life, these substances carry both potential and risk. I believe it's essential to approach them with mindfulness, accountability, and full awareness of the impact they can have on your mind, your body, and your life.

For me, the use of psychedelics, whether it's microdosing or macrodosing, has been a tool for deep self-reflection and growth. But I don't want anyone to think this is a one-size-fits-all approach. Psychedelics are not a solution to all of life's problems. It's crucial to approach them with caution and to respect the process. I encourage anyone who is considering using these substances to do their own research, understand the risks, and seek guidance from someone experienced or trained.

Part V

TYING UP LOOSE ENDS

In 2015, I took a significant step toward healing my relationship with my dad. Throughout college and my early NFL years, we'd share time together, he'd come to my games, we'd catch up, but there always seemed to be a distance between us, a gap I couldn't quite bridge. On Father's Day that year, I decided to write him a letter. I shared something I had come to realize: that both he and my mom had always done their best, and I held no grudges about the past. I told him I wanted a deeper relationship, one that would require effort from both of us.

That letter marked the beginning of a shift. Over time, we've grown closer. I even took up golf, one of his favorite hobbies, as a way to connect. When I played for Miami, I was able to spend more time with him and my little brothers, a gift I didn't take for granted. As I've spent more time with him, I've come to recognize parts of myself in him—both the strengths and the struggles. It's a reminder to keep evolving and strive to be a better version of myself, not just for me but as a way to honor my father and the lessons he's taught me.

I've come to realize that one of our greatest purposes in life is to build upon the foundation we've been given. Taking the lessons, both light and dark, from those who came before us and using them to shape something better for those who follow. For me, this means breaking certain cycles, showing my children how to be emotionally present, how to communicate with honesty, and how to navigate the world with compassion and resilience. It's about giving them the tools to face their own challenges, so they're not weighed down by the same burdens we once carried. In doing so, we leave behind not just a legacy of survival, but one of growth. One of creating a future that moves forward, informed by the past but not defined by it.

REFLECTION

Life begins at the end of your comfort zone.
—NEALE DONALD WALSCH

WE ALL HAVE THE POWER TO SHAPE THE WORLD around us. Every day we make choices; some keep things as they are, while others push for change. You don't need endless resources or time to make a difference. Small actions add up. Recycle. Conserve water. Plant trees. Support sustainable businesses. Buy local. Refuse to support brands that don't align with your values. Even conversations matter: talk about the changes you're making, inspire others, and build momentum.

Change starts with a single step. What's one thing you can commit to today? The future is shaped by what we choose to do now.

When it comes to politics, we often let those in power divide us.

What's it going to take for us to realize we're all in this together? No one politician can represent the entirety of a nation, let alone the world.

When you think about it: do you agree with every single decision made by our government? Of course not. So how can we judge one another based on the actions of political leaders, whether in our own country or abroad?

The sooner we realize that we're all connected, the sooner we can find common ground and start moving forward. We must stop letting the loudest, most extreme voices dictate the narrative. Real progress happens when we work together, with empathy, understanding, and a willingness to compromise.

Embracing life outside of my comfort zone has been the most significant choice I've made. The protest, therapy, healing. Attacking my fears, refining my identity. All of this was jump-started by me deciding to actively engage in life outside of my bubble.

Getting involved in the protest challenged me to learn about our shared history around the globe—capitalism, imperialism, militarism. And how those "isms" affect us today. Without this knowledge, we can't fight for ourselves. With it, we can slowly chop away at the system until it breaks in our favor.

Along the way I've realized how prioritizing our mental health is a part of being a revolutionary.

When we invest in ourselves, we all become activists, fighters, and changemakers. It's radical to confront our fears. It's radical to address the traumas of the past and make amends to move forward. Going down that road is no easy feat.

I commend those of us who have started the journey and encourage those who have not to understand that it's not too late. How do you want to spend your dash?

Reflecting on my past, I realize my younger self

would have dismissed my current values as *weak*. To be frank, the younger me would call me a pussy.

Embracing emotional intelligence, supporting the queer community, and expressing vulnerability were once dismissed in much of mainstream society. But challenging these tendencies sparked a metamorphosis. I've learned how vital it is to allow others to live authentically. And how much easier it is when I focus on my own stuff, not judging others or trying to control their behaviors.

As a man who played a violent and tough sport, I aim to redefine masculinity to include emotional intelligence—compassion, vulnerability, kindness, and authenticity. As well as resilience, dependability, and moral courage. It's past the time for men to be well-rounded individuals and partners; better sons and fathers. We need balance. Bottling up feelings or escaping through substances will not lead to fulfillment and sets the wrong example for our youth.

Recently, my sister India asked me, "What inspired you not to give up?" As I thought long and hard about the question, my eyes began to tear up. There were countless moments when I felt like throwing in the towel and walking away from the fight, shutting down, and disappearing. During some moments when I'd taken a step back to focus on my well-being, I lived with guilt, feeling like I was giving up. But I know now that taking care of myself was, in fact, a vital contribution to the movement.

I understand that life is a marathon and that's

how I need to approach it. No matter how bad I want things to change today, it's going to take time. I didn't quit before and I'm not going to start now. The resilience that our ancestors have shown, the joy through pain that we see every day in Gaza and around the world, inspire me to keep going. Some days it's sharing on social media, others it's marching in the streets. Sometimes it's a hard conversation with a loved one or even cutting them off and loving them from afar—but know that I'll always be committed. Eager to learn, love, and make an impact.

WHAT'S GOING ON NOW

Making the extraordinary ordinary.

As far as what I'm currently doing for work, I took a remote job with NFL Legends, which is our retired community. My job is to reach out and connect with our guys and inform them of our events and resources, and help in any way I can through the transition process. My hunger to serve outweighs anything I personally went through with the league. Especially when it comes to supporting the men I played with and those who came before me.

Initially I had a little PTSD going back to work for the NFL. Maybe it's in my head but I feel like I have to hold back parts of who I am in order to fit in with them. I struggle with the fact that there are so many rules in the corporate world. Ways we're expected to talk, act, and behave, and as you already know—rules aren't my thing. But I quickly realized that this group I get to work with is special, and it's made me feel like I've made the right decision. I've been able to transition smoothly out of the game and want to do whatever I can to help my brothers do the same.

There are twenty-three of us, all of different ages, experiences, and statuses. Coming together for one cause—to help our brothers. The wisdom shared in our meetings and side conversations is unmatched. And none of this would be possible without the thoughtful leadership and heart of those who guide our team. To me, this is invaluable and worth the little sacrifices I have to make in following the rules. Corporate Kenny has figured out how to play the game before, and I can do it again.

But I'm also in a different headspace. I now recognize that I control my reactions and where I focus my energy. And that if a place isn't harnessing the frequency I'm looking for, I can always respectfully step away.

I now get to live on my own terms and make my own schedule. That often means notifications off and devices away. I'm the closest thing living to a *Do Not Disturb* function. Early on, that too took some getting used to. Like most, I can feel a strong attachment to my device. Putting the phone down just to pick it back up. Or closing an app to immediately reopen it again.

Other patterns I've been paying attention to come from the body. I still feel urges of aggression and the need for nonsexual physical contact. That challenge of pushing the body and mind to their limits. I still feel that competitive desire and need to talk shit and get the juices flowing. Pretty quickly after leaving the league, I realized the gym would be my outlet. I still lift heavy and run sprints but have also added long distance, boxing, and HIIT to my routines.

When it comes to competition, I've had to tone it back a bit. I came from a place where losing was not accepted. In *anything*. If we played, I won. Or we played until I won. Especially if it was one-on-one. For my own sanity, I cut back on making everything a competition. Now if you call me out or challenge me, it's on. But in everyday life, I'm playing for fun . . . And winning is fun, so you get my drift. What I am really trying to say is that I've toned down the intensity. I've come to the realization that I'm only in competition with myself. I want to continue to evolve and build, but I've done the thing—achieved my dream. Everything else is icing on the cake.

While being unreachable and disconnected from the matrix forever sounds incredible, I do have other interests and goals. The luxury that I have now is that I don't have to press. Or expose my body to pain or injury to get there.

What I want to do next is focus even more on health and wellness. Sharing my story is a key step in that process. I also want to expand the Still Growing Summit, returning to cities I've played in and stopped at along the road trip.

Then I'd like to build a retreat and wellness facility, focused on healing. Through my journey, I've been exposed to many modalities and want to make them available and affordable for those willing to do the work. *Willing* is the key word. When I invested in my well-being, I saw returns. I wanted more, I wanted to change—I sought it out and put the work in. It was no miracle. Talk therapy, mindset work, and psychedelics have been effective for me, but who knows what the recipe is for you?

Practicing mindfulness, I've realized that in addition to those three pillars, I've also been making other daily deposits. The fuel I put into my body, the music I listen to, and how I spend my free time. I've cut out video games and begun to read more, journal more, play chess, and make visual art. I've found inspirational documentaries and informative podcasts to listen to. And I've started giving myself more credit for the little things I've accomplished.

With this I have reframed my self-care. Because self-care can be so many things. Showering, brushing my teeth, flossing, and moisturizing my skin—it's all self-care. Stretching, going to bed at a reasonable hour, hydrating. These are all investments in my body and quality of life; what matters is how we think about them, or if we even think about them at all.

In bed at night it is no longer, *What did I get done today?* It has become, *What am I grateful for? How did I show up? What made me smile? What are the little wins? How can I improve?*

I travel a lot these days, in search of experiences. Nature, food, and history. And I battle with sharing my experiences online. With so much darkness in the world, we need light—but sometimes sharing feels deeply inconsiderate. Here I am, peaking, while death and destruction obliterate around the globe.

When home, I'm reminded by friends and family of all the places "we've" been and how they are living through me. My aunty Debra recalls my trips like she was right there with me. And that warms my heart.

When I choose to share, it's with this in mind. When I'm radio silent, it's because nothing really matters.

IF ONE OF US AIN'T FREE,
WE ALL AIN'T FREE.

Acknowledgments

I am deeply grateful to the remarkable people whose support made this book a reality.

Dave Zirin, thank you for your guidance and encouragement as I worked on my first book. Your advice and your decision to publish the book on your Edge of Sports imprint helped make this journey smoother than I could have imagined.

To Rebecca, Max, Ivana, Omar, Noura, and Sara—thank you for your thoughtful feedback and for helping me shape this manuscript. Your insights challenged me to dig deeper and refine my ideas, making this work stronger with every revision.

To everyone who took the time to read early drafts or offer words of advice—your contributions, big or small, have left a lasting mark on this project.

To Akashic Books, whose belief in this work and commitment to its success has meant so much—I am grateful for your partnership, vision, and care in bringing this book to life. Your support of authors and dedication to bold, meaningful storytelling is something I deeply admire, and I'm proud to share this book with the world thanks to all of you.